Monumental Earthen Architecture in Early Societies

Technology and power display

Proceedings of the XVII UISPP World Congress (1–7 September, Burgos, Spain)

Volume 2 / Session B3

Edited by

Annick Daneels

Archaeopress Archaeology

ARCHAEOPRESS PUBLISHING LTD
Gordon House
276 Banbury Road
Oxford OX2 7ED

www.archaeopress.com

ISBN 978 1 78491 283 3
ISBN 978 1 78491 284 0 (e-Pdf)

© Archaeopress, UISPP and authors 2016

VOLUME EDITOR: Annick Daneels

SERIES EDITOR: The board of UISPP

SERIES PROPERTY: UISPP – International Union of Prehistoric and Protohistoric Sciences

The editing of this volume was funded by the Instituto Terra e Memória, Centro de Geociências UID/Multi/00073/2013, with the support of the Fundação para a Ciência e Tecnologia FCT/MEC)

KEY-WORDS IN THIS VOLUME: Monumental Architecture – Technology – Constructive Techniques – Power

UISPP PROCEEDINGS SERIES is a print on demand and an open access publication,
edited by UISPP through Archaeopress

BOARD OF UISPP: Jean Bourgeois (President), Luiz Oosterbeek (Secretary-General),
François Djindjian (Treasurer), Ya-Mei Hou (Vice President), Marta Arzarello (Deputy Secretary-General).
The Executive Committee of UISPP also includes the Presidents of all the international scientific
commissions (www.uispp.org)

BOARD OF THE XVII WORLD CONGRESS OF UISPP: Eudald Carbonell (Secretary-General),
Robert Sala I Ramos, Jose Maria Rodriguez Ponga (Deputy Secretary-Generals)

All rights reserved. No part of this book may be reproduced, or transmitted, in any form or by any means, electronic, mechanical, photocopying or otherwise, without the prior written permission of the copyright owners.

This book is available direct from Archaeopress or from our website www.archaeopress.com

Contents

List of Figures and Tables ii

Foreword to the XVII UISPP Congress Proceedings Series Edition iii
Luiz OOSTERBEEK

Introduction iv
Annick DANEELS

**Building Power: Earthen Monuments in the Construction of Elite Identities in
Pre-Columbian North America** 1
Melissa R. BALTUS

**Political and Technological Significance of the Monumental Earthen Architecture
of La Joya, on the Tropical Gulf Coast of Mexico** 13
Annick DANEELS

**Activity areas in two ceremonial centers of the Southern Brazilian Highlands:
relations between architecture and function** 21
Jonas Gregorio DE SOUZA

New data on the Neolithic ditches of the Tavoliere area (Apulia, Southern Italy) 31
Annamaria TUNZI & Tania QUERO

**First test for luminescence dating of ancient mud-brick buildings
from Northern Mesopotamia** 45
Jorge SANJURJO-SÁNCHEZ & Juan-Luis MONTERO FENOLLÓS

Traditional Architecture and Socio-Political Organization at Figuig Oasis, Morocco 53
Florencia Tatiana Azul Ultramar RAMÍREZ-RODRÍGUEZ

List of Figures and Tables

M. R. Baltus: Building Power: Earthen Monuments in the Construction of Elite Identities in Pre-Columbian North America

Figure 1. Cahokia and affiliated sites in the American Bottom region of the United States 2
Figure 2. Alternating light and dark soils as illustrated in lower one meter of Copper Mound 3 6
Figure 3. Homogenous grey silt lens in lower portion of Copper Mound 3 7
Figure 4. Examples of L-, T-, and circular shaped Cahokian structures 8

A. Daneels: Political and Technological Significance of the Monumental Earthen Architecture of La Joya, on the Tropical Gulf Coast of Mexico

Figure 1. Map with major earthen architecture sites cited in the text 14
Figure 2. La Joya, 3D reconstructions based on archaeological evidence 16

J. G. De Souza: Activity areas in two ceremonial centers of the Southern Brazilian Highlands: relations between architecture and function

Figure 1. Distribution of mound and enclosure complexes of the Taquara/Itararé Tradition 22
Figure 2. Structures of the site RS-PE-29 23
Figure 3. Sites RS-PE-31 (a) and Posto Fiscal (b) 24
Figure 4. Features in mound B, site Posto Fiscal 26

A. Tunzi & T. Quero: New data on the Neolithic ditches of the Tavoliere area (Apulia, Southern Italy)

Figure 1. Location of the sites of the Amendola Air Base and Masseria Montevergine 33
Figure 2. Aerial view of the Amendola ditch 34
Figure 3. Holes at the sides and the bottom of the Amendola ditch 34
Figure 4. Masses of blocks and rock fragments in the filling of the Amendola ditch 35
Figure 5. 'Guadone' *facies* potsherds (coarse and fine ware) from the Amendola site 36
Figure 6. Air photo interpretation of the features organisation at the Masseria Montevergine 38
Figure 7. View of some features at Masseria Montevergine 39
Figure 8. 'Masseria La Quercia' style potsherds and bone tools from Masseria Montevergine 40

J. Sanjurjo-Sánchez & J.-L. Montero Fenollós: First test for luminescence dating of ancient mud-brick buildings from Northern Mesopotamia

Figure 1. Map of Near East and location of the sites in the Middle Euphrates 49
Figure 2. Pictures of the sampled constructions 50
Table 1. Building materials, main raw materials, function and chronology of use by civilizations 47
Table 2. Ages obtained from the objects dated in the two sites studied 51

F. T. A. U. Ramírez-Rodríguez: Traditional Architecture and Socio-Political Organization at Figuig Oasis, Morocco

Figure 1. Location of Figuig Oasis in Morocco 54
Figure 2. Map of the Figuig Ksour 55
Figure 3. Walled gardens at Figuig Oasis 56
Figure 4. Ancient earthen watchtowers and rest of a defensive wall at Figuig Oasis 58
Figure 5. Settlement pattern in the old center of the Figuig Ksour 61

Foreword to the XVII UISPP Congress Proceedings Series Edition

Luiz OOSTERBEEK
Secretary-General

UISPP has a long history, starting with the old International Association of Anthropology and Archaeology, back in 1865, until the foundation of UISPP itself in Bern, in 1931, and its growing relevance after WWII, from the 1950's. We also became members of the International Council of Philosophy and Human Sciences, associate of UNESCO, in 1955.

In its XIVth world congress in 2001, in Liège, UISPP started a reorganization process that was deepened in the congresses of Lisbon (2006) and Florianópolis (2011), leading to its current structure, solidly anchored in more than twenty-five international scientific commissions, each coordinating a major cluster of research within six major chapters: Historiography, methods and theories; Culture, economy and environments; Archaeology of specific environments; Art and culture; Technology and economy; Archaeology and societies.

The XVIIth world congress of 2014, in Burgos, with the strong support of Fundación Atapuerca and other institutions, involved over 1700 papers from almost 60 countries of all continents. The proceedings, edited in this series but also as special issues of specialized scientific journals, will remain as the most important outcome of the congress.

Research faces growing threats all over the planet, due to lack of funding, repressive behavior and other constraints. UISPP moves ahead in this context with a strictly scientific programme, focused on the origins and evolution of humans, without conceding any room to short term agendas that are not rooted in the interest of knowledge.

In the long run, which is the terrain of knowledge and science, not much will remain from the contextual political constraints, as severe or dramatic as they may be, but the new advances into understanding the human past and its cultural diversity will last, this being a relevant contribution for contemporary and future societies.

This is what UISPP is for, and this is also why we are currently engaged in contributing for the relaunching of Human Sciences in their relations with social and natural sciences, namely collaborating with the International Year of Global Understanding, in 2016, and with the World Conference of the Humanities, in 2017.

The next two congresses of UISPP, in Melbourn (2017) and in Geneva (2020), will confirm this route.

Introduction

Annick DANEELS
Institute of Anthropological Research, National Autonomous University of Mexico.
Ciudad Universitaria, Delegación Coyoacán, México D.F., C.P. 04510, Mexico
annickdaneels@hotmail.com

The theme of the symposium is the archaeology of earthen architecture in pre- and protohistoric cultures, with an emphasis on constructive techniques and systems, and diachronic changes in those aspects. The main interest is in monumental architecture (not domestic), where it is better possible to appreciate the building strategies that show raw earth to be as noble a material as stone or wood, but with its very own characteristics which required the development of original solutions and construction techniques. The scope on monumental buildings also allows analyzing the political, social and economical factors that made such architecture a recognized expression of societal values and political power.

Many researchers, worldwide, are now interested in this topic, and their contributions are helping to reappraise the importance of this type of architecture, often considered inferior to its stone counterpart. Much of the investigation is centered on the civilizations of Mesopotamia, China and Perú, where major raw earth building traditions existed, that have been the object of study for a long time and are thus well published. The present symposium gathers six contributions from lesser known traditions, reaching from Neolithic Italy to present-day Morocco. The research interests of the papers are a sample of the wide variety of topics that can be broached from the study of earthen architecture. Baltus' Mississippian paper and Daneels' Mesoamerican one are similar in the way they link the act of building with sociopolitical strategy and ritual practice embedded in a particular worldview. The enclosures described by Tunzi and Quero in Italy and Gregorio in Brazil, though literally worlds apart in space, time and social context, represent two cases of fundamental archaeological research to ascertain the function of these little understood constructions. The work by Sanjurjo and Montero is a groundbreaking contribution to archaeometry, demonstrating that mud-bricks can be dated by thermoluminescence, allowing to define the moment of construction of buildings. Finally, the more anthropologically oriented work by Ramirez in Morocco correlates settlement pattern with sociopolitical organization, to propose the existence of a segmentary system surviving in a present-day oasis.

Building Power: Earthen Monuments in the Construction of Elite Identities in Pre-Columbian North America

Melissa R. BALTUS

University of Toledo, 2680G University Hall, Toledo, 43606 OH, USA

Melissa.Baltus@UToledo.Edu

Abstract

According to documents recorded by early European explorers, earthen platform mounds in the southeast United States were the domain of indigenous political and religious leaders. Rather than assuming a priori that these were elite spaces, current research into the earthen mounds of the late pre-Contact period (AD 1000-1400) of the American Midcontinent suggests these mounds were monuments of empowerment. Incorporating indigenous ontologies into the study of mound construction suggests that the act of gathering powerful elements (earth, water, fire) along with narrations of deep history (e.g., origin and ancestor-deity traditions) is an empowering act through which elite statuses were (re)constructed and maintained.

Keywords: *earthen architecture, Mississippian, power, elite*

Résumé

La construction du pouvoir: Monuments en terre pour construire l'identité des élites précolombiennes d'Amérique du Nord

Selon des documents enregistrés par les premiers explorateurs européens, les monticules de terre dans le sud-est des États-Unis étaient le domaine de dirigeants politiques et religieux indigènes. Plutôt que de supposer a priori que ce sont des espaces d'élite, les recherches actuelles sur les monticules de terre de la dernière période pré-contact (AD 1000-1400) du centre du continent nord-américain suggèrent que ces monticules sont des monuments de prise de pouvoir. L'intégration des ontologies autochtones dans l'étude de la construction du monticule suggère que le fait de recueillir des éléments puissants (terre, eau, feu) ainsi que des récits de l'histoire profonde (par exemple, les traditions d'origine et de déités-ancêtres) fassent que la construction soit un acte qui permette de (re)construire et d'entretenir le statut des élites.

Mots Clés: *architecture de terre, culture mississippienne, pouvoir, élite*

Introduction

The 16th century European explorers of the New World documented numerous Indigenous North American settlements where persons of political or religious significance lived and ruled from the summits of earthen monuments (Bourne ed. 1922; Varner, Varner 1951). More specifically, prominent earthen platform mounds in the North American Southeast supported residences of chiefs and members of their household as well as sacred temples (Varner, Varner 1951). The elite association of the mound-summit buildings identified by these early explorers is commonly extended by archaeologists to the earthen monuments upon which they stood, with the implicit or explicit assumption that mounds were elite spaces (Anderson 1997; Jennings 1952; Knight 1997; Pauketat 1993, 1994; Steponaitis 1986). The mound-building traditions of the 11th to 15th century Mississippian period both built upon and stood in opposition to earlier (pre-11th century) traditions of communal earthen constructions (though the communal nature of these earlier constructions may also need to be questioned, see Sassaman 2004). I investigate this apparent shift in practice and relationality from earthen monuments as communal constructions for the honored dead and earthen monuments as spaces of the living elite, focusing on the *processes* by which mounds became places of empowerment through the elements and buildings gathered within, at the 11th–14th century city of Cahokia (Figure 1).

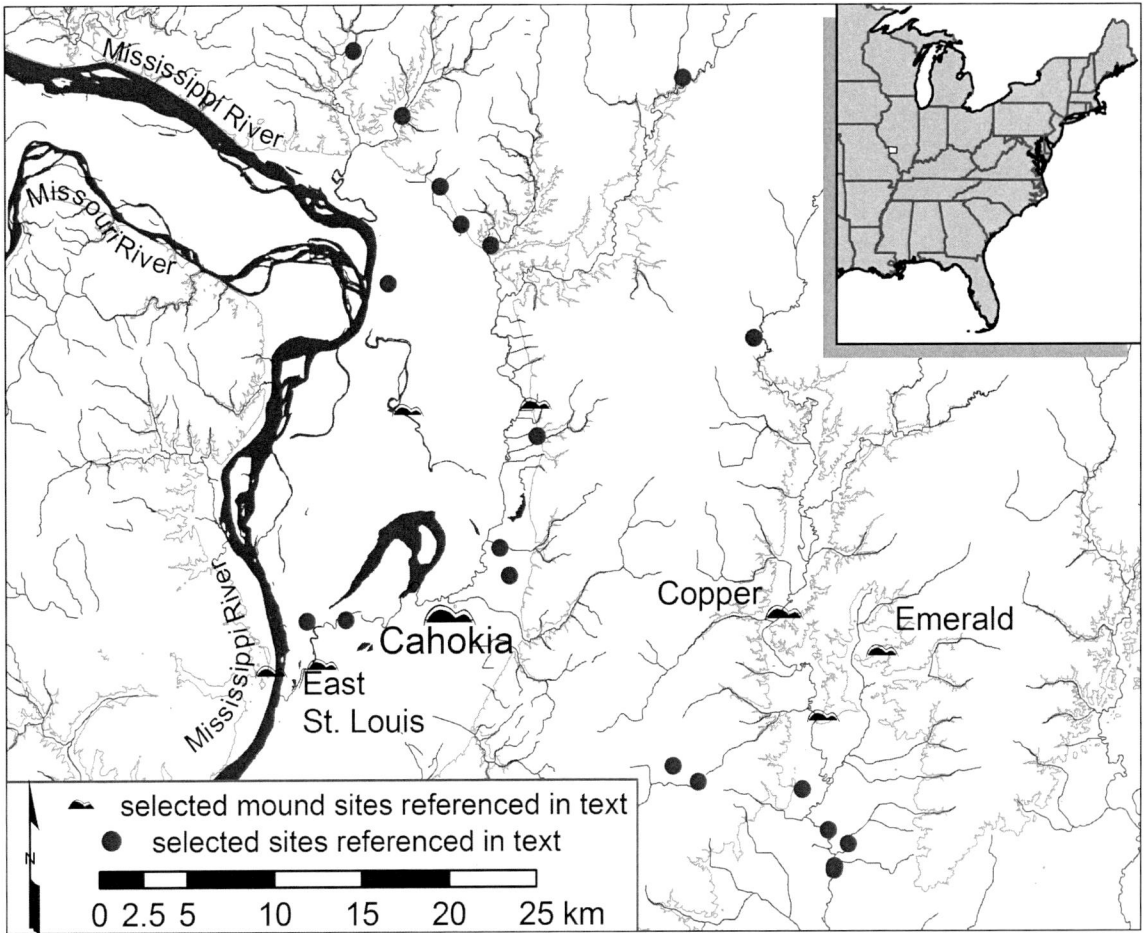

FIGURE 1. CAHOKIA AND AFFILIATED SITES IN THE AMERICAN BOTTOM REGION OF THE UNITED STATES.

Earthen Mound Traditions in the Eastern Woodlands

Pre-Mississippian mounds are often interpreted as material constructions of community identities, either containing venerated ancestors (e.g., Archaic shell mounds and burial mounds, Hopewell burial mounds) or marking corporate territory or clan identity (e.g., Late Woodland effigy mounds, ca. 700-1200 C.E.). Some Middle Archaic (ca. 6000-3000 B.C.E.) and Late Archaic (ca. 3000 B.C.E. – 1000 B.C.E.) mounds have been identified as platform mounds arranged around plaza spaces (Sassaman 2004; Saunders *et al*. 1994; Saunders *et al*. 1997; Saunders *et al*. 2000), suggesting that monumental earthen construction for purposes other than burial occurred as early as the Middle Archaic (Sassaman 2004). This mound-building tradition was referenced, replicated, and reconfigured in practice over the next 5000 years, continuing in varied intensity through the Woodland (ca. 1000 B.C.E. – 1050 C.E.) and Mississippian periods (ca. 1050-1500 C.E.) up to European contact. By the time of contact, earthen mounds were monuments supporting chiefly and priestly elite physically as well as politically, supposedly legitimizing their higher status through physical elevation (Dalan *et al*. 2003; Lewis *et al*. 1998).

This structural association between elevated physical position and symbolic legitimization of elites cannot be ascribed to as a natural given (*contra* Lewis *et al*. 1998:16 and Muller 1997:271); rather, this ontological link between elevation (especially in the context of earthen monuments) and power requires deconstruction through an investigation of the possible historical processes that *(re)created* that relationship in the specific context of the Mississippian Southeast. Additionally, the power of a particular social group should be considered beyond simply the authority to 'control' labor in the practice of mound construction, interrogating *why* they are authorized to do so. What processes are involved in the empowerment of a particular group? It is also necessary to consider that human labor is not the only force requiring control or engagement in the construction of earthen monuments. Soils, elements, supernatural beings and forces are likewise active agents in mound construction, whose participation – like that of humans – must be negotiated. Social power is not an innate given, but must continually be constructed, legitimized, and *accepted*. The entanglement between elite identities and earthen monuments in the Southeast noted at the time of European contact has been extended by researchers centuries into the past – to the initial construction of the Native American city of Cahokia during the 11th century C.E. While the construction of monuments for purposes of legitimizing power is not necessarily incompatible with the communal nature of construction practices, it is necessary to explore **how** earthen mound construction contributed to elite identities within the specific ontological context of the Eastern Woodlands of North America.

Earthen Monuments and Power at Cahokia

The initiation of mound building at Cahokia is often assumed to have been directed by already-powerful elites (Milner 1996, 1998), but this assumption ignores the ways in which those persons or groups gained that particular status in relation to earthen monumentality. Though earthen monuments and social inequalities likely extend even further into history (Sassaman 2004), Cahokia perhaps provides a starting point from which to interrogate the historic processes of elite-identity formation during the Mississippian period that culminated in those relationships between mounds and elites at the time of contact.

More recent excavations and re-analysis of past excavations into Cahokian earthen monuments provides evidence challenging this presumed elite power over earthen monument construction, especially where large public buildings are the foundational mound structures (A. Butler 2013; Zych 2013) or where mound interments consist of a broad demographic sample (Hedman, Hargrave 2014). This evidence suggests a communal nature of mound building at Cahokia and Cahokian-related sites in the Midwest as part of a newly introduced religious movement that united numerous diverse groups of people in shared religious practices that engage with cosmological powers, including earthen mound construction. Therefore, I suggest here that the process of empowerment of particular persons or groups of persons took place – at least in part – through increasingly entangled relationships with the cosmos as mediated through earthen monuments, including the construction materials, techniques, and the buildings incorporated within their history.

These processes of course need to be understood within the context of Cahokia. Cahokia was one of a kind, qualitatively and quantitatively different from all other Mississippian sites either contemporaneous with Cahokia or following in its wake. The first and biggest of Mississippian settlements – Cahokia was arguably the first urban experience north of Mexico (Pauketat 2004, 2007, 2011). Located in the wide floodplain of the Mississippi River Valley in the mid-continent, this city was upwards of 13 km^2 (more than 8 square miles) in size (Fowler 1997) and growing as new excavations in the area reveal a greater geographic extent (Emerson, Boles 2010). Though the acceptance of the urban nature of Cahokia has been debated (Welch 2004), the designation of 'city' is appropriate given the spatial extent and population estimates as compared to other New and Old World polities (see Pauketat 2007). The reluctance to consider Cahokia as an urban area retains echoes of the Moundbuilder Myth (see Mann 2006 for an indigenous perspective of this myth) and tends to be based on western standards of urbanization (Pauketat 2007; Welch 2004). Population estimates suggest that upwards of 16,000 people lived at Cahokia and its surrounding suburbs at its 12th century zenith (Pauketat 2004; Pauketat, Lopinot 1997), though these estimates are now outdated given survey and excavation results of the past decade (Emerson, Boles 2010). Mound construction at and around Cahokia began in earnest during the 10th century C.E. – shortly before, or more accurately in conjunction with, the initiation of this population coalescence (Dalan *et al.* 2003). Small hamlets, farmsteads, and a series of shrine sites extended into the floodplain and uplands beyond the city (see Figure 1) (Alt 2006a; Emerson 1997). The inhabitants of Cahokia and the surrounding suburbs included diverse groups of immigrants drawn to the city from other locations in the mid-continent (Alt 2006b; Slater *et al.* 2014). Based on evidence for novel ceremonialism – including earthen platform mound construction – a new religious movement is suggested to be the factor which drew people to Cahokia (Pauketat 2013).

Early Mississippian mound construction at Cahokia has often been portrayed as a form of 'co-optation' or 'appropriation' of the tradition of mound-building as a means of legitimizing the ruling elite (Dalan *et al.* 2003). Citing the complicated dynamics of power relations, Dalan and colleagues (2003: 174) suggest that monuments like earthen mounds became 'places where changing power relations could be played out.' At the same time, however, the communal act of constructing these monuments has been demonstrated to be a means of building community-identity. Practices of mound-building and renewal helped unite and hold together disparate groups as a community through shared action and belief (Pauketat, Alt 2003; Zych 2013). This communal construction of mounds contributed to what Dalan and colleagues (2003:174) call an 'empowerment by the masses' of an elite subset.

The *a priori* elite nature of Mississippian mounds is here called into question. Rather than places of static meaning, mounds – like all other social constructions – should be conceptualized as dynamic. Mounds are ever in a perpetual state of becoming (Pauketat 2007); changing in use, perception, and meaning throughout time and space. I suggest that the power of earthen mounds does not derive from an inherent 'eliteness', but rather Mississippian mounds were co-creative of persons of elite status.

This argument requires consideration of two important details of Mississippian mounds 1) the pattern or 'recipe' of Mississippian mound construction and 2) the historical trajectory of their association with particular structures. These lines of evidence need also be compared with earlier traditions of earthen monument construction to question the linkage between mounds and priestly/chiefly elite.

Relationships of Power: Elements, Buildings, People

More recent theories embracing alternate ontologies and aspects of practice and relationality have reconfigured concepts like power (Alberti *et al.* 2011). I use relationality here to refer to the qualities of or degrees of 'institutional, imaginative, and…interpersonal' relationships that humans form with other-than-humans through their daily interactions (Merlan 2013: 637). Among many (arguably most) non-Western and pre-industrial societies, including Indigenous North American groups, the world is inhabited by a variety of sentient beings, only some of whom are humans (as recorded in works such as Bailey 1995; Hallowell 1960, 1975; see also Hill 2012). Other social agents, with whom humans enter into relationships, include ancestors, deities, animals, natural and supernatural phenomena, forces of nature, elements, and even objects (Deloria 1973; Neihardt 1979). Many Native North American groups frequently conceptualized power as a dispersed force or animating factor within the visible and invisible world (Bailey 1995; Fletcher, La Flesche 1992; Hudson 1976). This power can be situated within numerous elements, beings, or places on a contextual basis. Two elements in particular – earth and fire – are considered to be fundamental animate and animating powers of the universe (Dorsey 1894; Howard 1981; Pauketat 2014), and are significant elements of mound construction in Native North America. I would argue that water – another key animate force as well as locus of animating power (Bouguerra 2005; Sassaman 2012) was likewise an empowering element of earthen monument construction.

Timothy Pauketat describes earthen mounds as 'imaginaries' – portals that provide access to other worlds through their powerful combinations of elements (Pauketat 2014). From this perspective of people actively engaging with powerful cosmic forces, it is in the creation and maintenance of earthen monuments that their significance lies, rather than necessarily as 'finished' monuments (Pauketat 2008; see also Dalan *et al.* 2003:150). Through the act of building with earth, water, and fire, people engaged with worlds beyond the physical and temporal present (Pauketat 2014).

This ontological turn in archaeology thus challenges scientists to view/accept these imaginaries as people in the past may have experienced them. This challenge incorporates both the aesthetic properties of earthen monument construction, as well as the engineering properties that may have been considered elemental to particular soils. These engineering properties may have included 'invisible' forces added to these mounds through practices of dancing/stomping, touching/manipulating the soil, and offerings of tobacco or other significant substances. Perhaps even the act of digging into the earth or scooping soil from below the water may have incorporated metaphysical engineering properties into these monuments (see below).

Earthen mound construction in North America has a deep history, encompassing nearly seven millennia, and extending geographically throughout the Eastern Woodlands and onto the Great Plains. The elite nature of mounds at the time of contact has certainly problematized the Archaic period mounds at Watson Brake and Poverty Point (Sassaman 2004). The Archaic period is supposedly a time of egalitarian hunting and gathering societies (though see Sassaman 2004) which contradicts with the presumption that mound construction was exacted by an elite subset of the population. This same contradiction follows through the subsequent millennia of Woodland burial and effigy mounds. In fact, we may call into question Western assumptions that inclusion of an individual within burial mounds simply reflected the status held by that person while alive. Status – like all social identities – is dynamic, constructed, and transcendent. I say transcendent as death among Indigenous North Americans is merely an aspect of life, a movement into another world in which relational identities continue to be transformed (Baires 2014; Deloria 1973). In this manner, status may be *conferred* via burial in mound contexts – status that may or may not have been a significant aspect of a person's *living* identity but perhaps an aspect of their identity in the afterlife.

Arguing that the acts of mound construction were not necessarily elite-driven does not mean to imply that mound building groups were somehow 'less complex' – rather the opposite; that a series of complicated and complex relationships with the earth, elements, and the cosmos were entangled and managed through the layers of soil, fire, water, and buildings that were added to each mound. Evidence at Cahokia and Cahokia-related sites suggest that mound construction began as a communal process, one tied to concerns of cosmological balance and earth-renewal associated with a new religious order (Pauketat 2013; Zych 2013). Over time, however, this new religion appears to have become more politicized as suggested by increasingly standardized ritual practices, and tied to a burgeoning new class of elite identities through their closer relationship with cosmological power gathered and manipulated in special buildings and earthen monuments (Baltus 2014; Emerson 1997; Pauketat 1997).

This new Cahokian religion appears to have engaged with shared elements of a Native American cosmology recorded in ethnohistories of the Eastern Woodlands and Southeast. This cosmology entailed a tripartite conceptualization of the universe: an Upper World, and Under World, and a 'here' or Middle World (Bailey 2005; Hall 1997; Hudson 1976; Swanton 2001 [1931]). Robert Hall (1997) and many others have connected Eastern Woodlands North American world origin stories to mound construction. Most specifically the Earth Diver Myth credits the creation of the earth to an ingenious deity-animal - usually one who can transcend boundaries between the Middle and the Under Worlds (i.e., duck, muskrat, crawfish). At the watery beginning of the world, this being dove beneath the surface of the water, bringing sediments from below and piling it up to create the earth (Fletcher, La Flesche 1992).

A variety of construction techniques have been identified in Cahokian mounds, some of which bring these earth-diver histories to life. These include incremental layers or blanket mantles, sod blocks, soil blocks, silt lenses, and individual basket-loads. While individual mound strata provide a history of their construction and use (Pauketat *et al*. 2010), Mississippian mound construction typically follows a pattern or 'recipe' involving soils of alternating colors and/or textures (Figure 2). Oftentimes, these alternating zones are small and incremental near the base of the mound with larger zones of

FIGURE 2. ALTERNATING LIGHT AND DARK SOILS AS ILLUSTRATED IN LOWER ONE METER OF COPPER MOUND 3.

basket-loaded soils or thicker mantles of soils. Others have suggested that the incremental layers of alternating colors may be chosen for aesthetics (Dalan *et al.* 2003; Pursell 2004, 2013) engineering principles (Dalan *et al.* 2003), and that particular soils were chosen for symbolic purposes (Knight 1989; Milner 2004:125-126; Sabo 1985), while Pauketat (2008, 2013) has contended that these alternating colors were a means of *physically* balancing oppositions to bring order to the cosmos.

In addition to alternating light and dark soils, Cahokian mounds often incorporated oppositional forces of fire and water. I, along with Sarah Baires, have argued previously that the powerful element of fire was used to mediate places of power in the Cahokian world (Baltus, Baires 2012). This transformative element was recognized by Native Americans as a force of life and transcendence and was often incorporated in cleansing rituals among various Eastern Woodlands and Plains groups (Bailey 1995; Grantham 2002; La Flesche 1939; Radin 1970). Numerous Cahokian mounds show evidence for thin lenses of ash, charcoal, and in situ burning (Baltus 2014; Pauketat *et al.* 2010; Smith 1969), many of which appear to be related to incinerated structures of the types discussed below. These buildings were powerful places by virtue of their role in housing religious practices that gathered dispersed cosmological powers, or places guarding and protecting powerful religious paraphernalia. As such, these spaces required cleansing both physically and spiritually via fire and layers of earth to mediate their power (Baltus, Baires 2012; see also Knight 1989, Waring 1968).

In other cases, water and water-laid silts were used to mediate, construct, or in some other manner mark important places. A small mound in the Grand Plaza at Cahokia (Mound 49) exhibited thin lenses of water-sorted silts and sands near its base (Pauketat *et al.* 2010). Two shrine sites in the uplands east of Cahokia exhibit intentional in-silting of special buildings and monumental marker posts, left open to a series of rain events upon their termination and visible as alternating zones of water-sorted silts and intentionally packed soils (Otten *et al.* 2007; Pauketat 2013; Pauketat personal communication 2014). The repeated sequence of water-sorted silts and mixed light and dark soils packed into these features highlights the intentional inclusion of these soils. The pattern found in unique features at different sites in both floodplain and upland locations precludes interpretation as incidental or merely taphonomic.

My own recent excavations in a platform mound at another upland shrine site east of Cahokia, known as the Copper site (see Figure 1), revealed not just water-deposited silts, but submerged sediments that were intentionally collected and deposited within the mound (Baltus 2014). Minimally, two

FIGURE 3. HOMOGENOUS GREY SILT LENS IN LOWER PORTION OF COPPER MOUND 3.

zones of silt (each 10 cm thick) at the base of this mound do not exhibit banding associated with rain-based erosional silt zones, but represent homogenous gray silt deposits (Figure 3). These silts do not occur in the natural subsoil at this site, but rather were collected from under-water sources (likely the nearby creek), sorted, and packed into the base of the mound. Water is an important component in the creation and renewal of the earth, as noted above. Among agricultural societies, water in the form of rain would have meant life. Among the Pawnee (Caddoan speakers of the Great Plains and Southeastern US) the Earth and life upon it were created through a succession of thunderstorms; likewise, thunder heralds the spring (seasonal renewal of the earth) tied to the beginning of the ceremonial calendar (Fletcher, La Flesche 1992; Weltfish 1965).

The incorporation of powerful life-giving elements like fire and water into earthen monuments was part of a series of communally-based religious practices allowing multiple members of the community to engage with powers of the earth. The addition of gathered soils (e.g., subaqueous sediments) and basket loads of earth was likely a widely-participated in event, not restricted to select members of the community. However, the manipulation of these elements within a *sacred space* was likely under the purview of particular religious persons (see Bailey 1995; Hudson 1976; Weltfish 1965).

The second empowering feature of earthen monuments of the Mississippian period involves the incorporation of important buildings into mound construction. Excavations into numerous platform mounds at and around Cahokia reveal a series of structures erected on various surfaces throughout the mounds (Baltus 2014; Moorehead 2000; Pauketat 1993; Pauketat *et al.* 2010; Smith 1969).

Particular buildings below and on mound surfaces at Cahokia are themselves innovations, akin to traditional public and religious structures. These building varieties include rectangular single-post structures that perhaps began as non-secular buildings but were reconceptualized as Cahokian temples, circular structures serving as formal sweatlodges, and L- or T-shaped buildings that were likely priestly residences with an alcoves for housing sacred paraphernalia (Figure 4) (Alt 2006a; Emerson 1997; Pauketat 2004). Many of these structures were burned prior to being encapsulated with layers of earth, and oftentimes mirror, or cite, the location of previous buildings below (Pauketat 1993; Zych 2013). The citationality (as an aspect of performance and practice, see J. Butler 1993) of these building sequences, in which each construction episode references in location or orientation the building below (sensu Antrim 2012 and Inomata, Tsukamoto 2014), suggests that subsequent buildings drew power from, and perhaps reanimated, the previous buildings or features below.

FIGURE 4. EXAMPLES OF L-, T-, AND CIRCULAR SHAPED CAHOKIAN STRUCTURES.

In addition to the single post temples, sweatlodges, and priestly residences, charnel structures formed the final important buildings incorporated into mound constructions. Charnel houses are identified at the base, upper surface, and apron extensions of mortuary mounds at Cahokia (Alt, Pauketat 2007; Baires 2014; Fowler *et al*. 1999; Moorehead 2000). These mortuary facilities were initially believed to have housed only important individuals – again with the assumption that burial status reflected status in life (Peebles, Kus 1977). A recent reanalysis of isotopic evidence from burials of co-mingled men, women, and children from one principal mound at Cahokia (Mound 72) demonstrates the interred individuals derived from Cahokia and outside of Cahokia (Slater *et al*. 2014). These co-mingled burials are more likely part of the process of community-creation through ancestors common to Cahokia as a whole (i.e., the physical creation of a community of diverse groups of people by gathering their ancestors together in a collective burial). Significantly, these collective burials are foundational elements of early mound constructions at Cahokia highlighting a community-based and community-constructing practice in the founding years of Cahokia (Baires 2014).

Conclusion

Temples, sweatlodges, priestly residences, and mortuary features are found throughout Cahokia and Cahokia-related sites. Why were particular buildings and burials encapsulated within mound construction and others not? Following Pauketat (2008) and Baltus and Baires (2012), I suggest that specific buildings were locations of particularly powerful occurrences, ones that required mediation through the balancing effect of oppositional forces of fire and water, light and dark earth. Further, these practices of deposition and layering cite and enact creation narratives at these specific places, simultaneously creating an origin place and place of gathered power – as suggested by Pauketat (2014) in his assessment of mounds as portals.

I further contend that these mounds-as-portals were places of empowerment, where a new religious authority, and thus a new type of elite subcommunity, was constructed at Cahokia. From a relational perspective, the ability to manipulate powerful elements and engage with powerful entities in the construction of these monuments may have led to the creation of particular groups of people as elite. Pauketat (2007:42) has argued that the act of earthen mound building effectively brought the Cahokian political institutions into being. Drawing on this transformative state of 'becoming', I argue that the elite associations of Southeastern earthen platform mounds as seen at the time of European contact had its roots earlier in the Mississippian period – during its infant stages at the city of Cahokia. Further engagement with these increasingly powerful places by certain personages – for example persons charged with maintaining the charnel structures, responsible for curating religious paraphernalia, or for leading ceremonials that renew the earth – increasingly empowered those persons. The argument presented here does not deny a relationship between powerful elites and earthen monuments, but focuses on the historic processes through which that relationship and the social status developed. Rather than persons residing on mounds because they were powerful, these persons became powerful through their engagement with those monuments.

Bibliography

ALBERTI, A.; FOWLES, S.; HOLBRAAD, M.; MARSHALL, Y.; WHITMORE, C. 2011. 'Worlds Otherwise': Archaeology, Anthropology, and Ontological Difference. Current Anthropology 52(6), p. 896-912.

ALT, S. M. 2006a. Cultural Pluralism and Complexity: Analyzing a Cahokian Ritual Outpost. Unpublished Ph.D. Dissertation, Department of Anthropology. Urbana-Champaign:University of Illinois.

ALT, S. M. 2006b. The Power of Diversity: The Roles of Migration and Hybridity in Culture Change. In Butler, B. M.; Welch, P. D. eds., Leadership and Polity in Mississippian Society. Center for Archaeological Investigations. Carbondale: Southern Illinois University, p. 289-308.

ALT, S. M.; PAUKETAT, T. 2007. Sex and the Southern Cult. In A. King ed., The Southeastern Ceremonial Complex. Tuscaloosa: University of Alabama Press. p. 232-250.

ANDERSON, D. G. 1997. The Role of Cahokia in the Evolution of Southeastern Mississippian Society. In Pauketat, T. R.; Emerson, T. E., eds., Cahokia: Domination and Ideology in the Mississippian World. Lincoln: University of Nebraska Press. p. 248-268.

ANTRIM, Z. 2012. Routes and Realms: The Power of Place in the Early Islamic World. Oxford: University of Oxford Press. 240 p.

BAILEY, G. A. 1995. The Osage and the Invisible World: From the Works of Francis La Flesche. Norman: University of Oklahoma Press. 344 p.

BAIRES, S. E. 2014. Cahokia's Origins: Religion, Complexity and Ridge-top Mortuaries in the Mississippi River Valley. Unpublished Ph.D. Dissertation, Department of Anthropology. Urbana-Champaign: University of Illinois.

BALTUS, M. R. 2014. Transforming Material Relationships: 13th Century Revitalization of Cahokian Religious-Politics. Unpublished Ph.D. Dissertation, Department of Anthropology. Urbana-Champaign: University of Illinois.

BALTUS, M. R.; BAIRES, S. E. 2012. Elements of Ancient Power in the Cahokian World. Journal of Social Archaeology 12(2), p. 167-192.

BOUGUERRA, L. 2005. Water: Symbolism and Culture, Les Rapports de l'Institut Veolia Environnement, no. 5.

BOURNE, E. G. [editor] 1922. Narratives of the Career of Hernando de Soto in the Conquest of Florida: As Told by a Knight of Elvas, and in a relation by Luys Hernandez de Biedma, Factor of the Expedition. Translated by Buckingham Smith together with an account of de Soto's expedition based on the diary of Rodrigo Ranjel, his private secretary, translated from Oviedo's Historia General y Natural de las Indias. New York: Allerton Book Co.

BUTLER, A. J. 2013. Mississippians in the 'Boonies': New Investigations and Insights at the Collins Site. Poster presented at the annual meeting of the Midwest Archaeological Conference, October 24-27, Columbus, Ohio.

BUTLER, J. 1993. Bodies that Matter: On the Discursive Limits of 'Sex'. New York: Routledge. xi + 284 p.

DALAN, R. A.; HOLLEY, G. R.; WOODS, W. I.; WATTERS, JR., H. W.; KOEPKE, J. A. 2003. Envisioning Cahokia: A Landscape Perspective. DeKalb: Northern Illinois University Press. 241 p.

DELORIA, V., JR. 1973. God is Red. New York: Grosset & Dunlap. 376 p.

DORSEY, J. O. 1894. A Study of Siouan Cults. In Eleventh Annual Report of the Bureau of Ethnology, pp. 351-554. Washington, DC: Smithsonian Institution.

EMERSON, T. E. 1997. Cahokia and the Archaeology of Power. Tuscaloosa: University of Alabama Press.

EMERSON, T. E.; BOLES, S. L. 2010. Contextualizing Flint Clay Cahokia Figures at the East St. Louis Mound Center. Illinois Archaeology: Journal of the Illinois Archaeological Survey, 22, p. 473-490.

FLETCHER, A. C.; LA FLESCHE, F. 1992. The Omaha Tribe. Lincoln: University of Nebraska Press. 643 p.

FOWLER, M. L. 1997. The Cahokia Atlas: A Historical Atlas of Cahokia Archaeology. Revised edition. Illinois Transportation Archaeological Research Program, Studies in Archaeology, No. 2. Urbana: University of Illinois. 267 p.

GRANTHAM, B. 2002. Creation Myths and Legends of the Creek Indians. Gainesville: University Press of Florida. xi + 337 p.

HALL, R. L. 1997. Archaeology of the Soul: North American Indian Belief and Ritual. Chicago: University of Illinois Press. xiv + 222 p.

HALLOWELL, A. I. 1975. Ojibwa Ontology, Behavior, and World View. In Tedlock, D.; Tedlock, B., eds., Teachings from the American Earth: Indian Religion and Philosophy. New York: Liveright, p. 141-178.

HEDMAN, K. M.; HARGRAVE, E. A. 2014. Cahokia Mound 72: Reinterpreting Meaning. Paper presented at the annual meeting of the Midwest Archaeological Conference, October 2-4, Champaign, IL.

HILL, E. 2012. The Nonempirical Past: Enculturated Landscapes and Other-than-Human Persons in Southwest Alaska. Arctic Anthropology 49(2), p. 41-57.

HOWARD, J. H. 1981. Shawnee! The Ceremonialism of a Native Indian Tribe and its Cultural Background. Athens: Ohio University Press. 454 p.

HUDSON, C. M. 1976. The Southeastern Indians. Knoxville: University of Tennessee Press.

INOMATA, T.; TSUKAMOTO, K. 2014. Gathering in an Open Space: Introduction to Mesoamerican Plazas. In Tsukamoto, K.; Inomata, T., eds., Mesoamerican Plazas: Arenas of Community and Power. Tucson: University of Arizona Press, p. 3-15.

JENNINGS, J. D. 1952. Prehistory of the Lower Mississippi Valley. In J. B. Griffin, ed., Archaeology of Eastern United States. Chicago: University of Chicago Press, p. 256-271.

KNIGHT, V. J., JR. 1989. Symbolism of Mississippian Mounds. In Wood, P. H.; Waselkov, G. A.; Hatley, M. T., eds., Powhatan's Mantle: Indians in the Colonial Southeast. Lincoln: University of Nebraska Press, p. 279-291.

KNIGHT, V. J., JR. 1997. Some Developmental Parallels between Cahokia and Moundville. In Pauketat, T. R.; Emerson, T. E., eds., Cahokia: Domination and Ideology in the Mississippian World. Lincoln: University of Nebraska Press, p. 229-247.

LA FLESCHE, F. 1939. War Ceremony and Peace Ceremony of the Osage Indians. Bureau of American Ethnology Bulletin 101. Washington D.C.: Smithsonian Institution.

LEWIS, R. B.; STOUT, C.; WESSON, C. B. 1998. The Design of Mississippian Towns. In Lewis, R. B.; Stout, C., eds., Mississippian Towns and Sacred Spaces: Searching for an Architectural Grammar. Tuscaloosa: University of Alabama Press, p. 1-21.

MANN, B. A. 2006. Native Americans, Archaeologists, and the Mounds. New York: Peter Lang Publishing, Inc. xxvi + 520 p.

MERLAN, F. 2013. Theorizing Relationality: A Response to the Morphys. American Anthropologist, 115(4), p. 637-638.

MILNER, G. R. 1996. Development and Dissolution of a Mississippian Society in the American Bottom, Illinois. In Scarry, J. F., ed., Political Structure and Change in the Prehistoric Southeastern United States. Gainesville: University Press of Florida, p. 27-52.

MILNER, G. R. 1998. The Cahokia Chiefdom: The Archaeology of a Mississippian Society. Washington, D.C.: Smithsonian Institution Press. xvi + 216 p.

MOOREHEAD, W. K. 2000. The Cahokia Mounds. Edited and with introduction by Kelly, J. E. Tuscaloosa: University of Alabama Press. xvi + 432 p.

MULLER, J. 1997. Mississippian Political Economy. New York: Plenum Press. xiii + 455 p.

NEIHARDT, J. G. 1979. Black Elk Speaks: Being the Life Story of a Holy Man of the Oglala Sioux As told through John G. Neihardt. Lincoln: University of Nebraska Press.

OTTEN, S. E.; BALTUS, M. R.; PAUKETAT, T. R. 2007. New Evidence of Temple Ritual and Earthen Symbolism at the Pfeffer Site. Paper presented at the annual meeting of the Southeastern Archaeological Conference, October 31 – November 3, Knoxville, Tennessee.

PAUKETAT, T. R. 1993. Temples for Cahokia Lords: Preston Holder's 1955-1956 Excavations of Kunnemann Mound. Memoirs, Museum of Anthropology, No. 26. Ann Arbor: University of Michigan. 166 p.

PAUKETAT, T. R. 1994. The Ascent of Chiefs: Cahokia and Mississippian Politics in Native North America. Tuscaloosa: The University of Alabama Press. 237 p.

PAUKETAT, T. R. 1997. Cahokian Elite Ideology and the Mississippian Cosmos. In Pauketat, T. R.; Emerson, T. E., eds., Cahokia: Domination and Ideology in the Mississippian World. Lincoln: University of Nebraska Press, p. 190-228.

PAUKETAT, T. R. 2004. Ancient Cahokia and the Mississippians. Cambridge: Cambridge University Press. 218 p.

PAUKETAT, T. R. 2007. Chiefdoms and other Archaeological Delusions. New York: Altamira Press. 257 p.

PAUKETAT, T. R. 2008. Founders' Cults and the Archaeology of Wa-kan-da. In Mills, B., ed., Memory Work: the Archaeologies of Material Practice. Santa Fe: School for Advanced Research Press, p. 61-80.

PAUKETAT, T. R. 2011. City of Earth and Wood: New Cahokia and its Material-Historical Implications. Paper prepared for A World of Cities conference at the Institute for the Study of the Ancient World, March 25-26, New York University, NY.

PAUKETAT, T. R. 2013. An Archaeology of the Cosmos: Rethinking Agency and Religion in Ancient America. New York: Routledge. 230 p.

PAUKETAT, T. R. 2014. From Memorials to Imaginaries in the Monumentality of Ancient North America. In Osborne, J. F., ed., Approaching Monumentality in Archaeology, IEMA Proceedings, Volume 3. Albany: State University of New York Press, p. 431-446.

PAUKETAT, T. R.; ALT, S. M. 2003. Mounds, Memory, and Contested Mississippian History. In Van Dyke, R. M.; Alcock, S. E., eds., Archaeologies of Memory. Oxford: Blackwell, p. 151-179.

PAUKETAT, T. R.; LOPINOT, N. H. 1997. Cahokian Population Dynamics. In Pauketat, T. R.; Emerson, T.E., eds., Cahokia: Domination and Ideology in the Mississippian World. Lincoln: University of Nebraska Press, p. 103-123.

PAUKETAT, T. R.; REES, M. A.; VANDERWARKER, A. M.; PARKER, K. E. 2010. Excavations into Cahokia's Mound 49. Illinois Archaeology 22(2), p. 397-436.

PEEBLES, C. S.; KUS, S. M. 1977. Some archaeological correlates of ranked societies. American Antiquity 42, p.421-448.

PURSELL, C. 2004. Geographic Distribution and Symbolism of Colored Mound Architecture in the Mississippian Southeast. Paper presented at the 61st Annual Meeting of the Southeastern Archaeological Conference and 50th Annual Meeting of the Midwestern Archaeological Conference, 20-23 Oct, St. Louis, MO.

PURSELL, C. 2013. Colored monuments and sensory theater among the Mississippians. In Day, J., ed., Making Senses of the Past: Toward a Sensory Archaeology. Center for Archaeological Investigations Occasional Paper No. 40, Carbondale: Southern Illinois University, p. 69-89.

RADIN, P. 1970 [1923]. The Winnebago Tribe. Originally published as a paper accompanying the 37th Annual Report of the U.S. Bureau of Ethnology to the Secretary of the Smithsonian Institution, 1915-1916. New York: Johnson Reprint Corporation. 560 p.

REED, N. A.; BENNETT, J. W.; PORTER, J. W. 1968. Solid core drilling of Monks Mound: technique and findings. American Antiquity 33(2), p. 137-148.

SABO, G., III 1985. Mound-building as Material Symbolism: An example from the Western Ozark Highland. Paper presented at the Society for American Archaeology annual meeting, May, Denver, CO.

SASSAMAN, K. 2004. Complex Hunter-Gatherers in Evolution and History: A North American Perspective. Journal of Archaeological Research 12(3), p. 227-280.

SASSAMAN, K. 2012. Futurologists Look Back. Archaeologies: Journal of the World Archaeological Congress 8(3), p. 250-268.

SLATER, P. A.; HEDMAN, K. M.; EMERSON, T. E. 2014. Immigrants at the Mississippian polity of Cahokia: Strontium isotope evidence for population movement. Journal of Archaeological Science 44:117-127.

SMITH, H. M. 1969. The Murdock Mound. In Fowler M. L., ed., Explorations into Cahokia Archaeology, Illinois Archaeological Survey Bulletin 7. Urbana: University of Illinois, p. 49-88.

STEPONAITIS, V. P. 1986. Prehistoric archaeology in the southeastern United States, 1970-1985. Annual Review of Anthropology 15, p. 363-404.

SWANTON, J. R. 2001 [1931]. Source Material for the Social and Ceremonial Life of the Choctaw Indians. Tuscaloosa: The University of Alabama Press. x + 282 p.

VARNER, J. G.; VARNER, J. J. [translators] 1951. The Florida of the Inca. London: Thomas Nelson and Sons, Ltd. xlv + 655 p.

WARING, A. J., JR. 1968. The Southern Cult and Muskhogean Ceremonial. In Williams, S., ed., The Waring Papers: The Collected Works of Antonio J. Waring, Jr. Peabody Museum Papers 58. Cambridge: Harvard University, p. 30-69.

WELCH, P. 2004. How Early were Cities in the Eastern United States? Journal of Urban History 30(4), p. 594-603.

WELTFISH, G. 1965. The Lost Universe. New York: Basic Books, Inc. xx + 506 p.

ZYCH, T. J. 2013. The Construction of a Mound and a New Community: An Analysis of the Ceramic and Feature Assemblages from the Northeast Mound at the Aztalan Site. Unpublished Master's Thesis, Department of Anthropology. Milwaukee: University of Wisconsin.

Political and Technological Significance of the Monumental Earthen Architecture of La Joya, on the Tropical Gulf Coast of Mexico

Annick DANEELS

Instituto de Investigaciones Antropológicas, Universidad Nacional Autónoma de México,
Ciudad Universitaria, Delegación Coyoacán, México D.F., C.P. 04510, Mexico
annickdaneels@hotmail.com

Abstract

Recent investigations at one of the thousands of pre-Columbian mounded sites along the southern Gulf coast of Mexico demonstrate the development of monumental urban constructions made of raw earth, using innovative building techniques and associated with lavish consecration deposits. The emergence of this architecture has to be understood within the context of a complex, probably state-level society, in terms of its cultural antecedents, the degree of expert knowledge, amount of labour input required, and the ideological and ritual programs by which the artificially created spaces were sacralized.

Keywords: *Mesoamerican archaeology, adobe, human sacrifice, Veracruz*

Résumé

Importance politique et technologique de l'architecture monumentale en terre de La Joya, sur la côte tropicale du Golfe du Mexique

Des recherches récentes dans un des milliers de sites précolombiens sur la Côte du Golfe du Mexique démontrent le développement de constructions monumentales en terre crue, caractérisé par des techniques constructives originales et des offrandes de consécration. L'apparition de ce type d'architecture ne peut être compris que dans le contexte d'une société complexe, probablement d'organisation étatique, si l'on prend en compte ses antécédents culturels, le degré d'expertise, la quantité de main d'œuvre requise, et les programmes idéologiques et rituels employés pour sacraliser les espaces artificiellement construits.

Mots Clés: *archéologie mésoaméricaine, adobe, sacrifice humain, Véracruz*

Introduction

Only recently has the concept of a Mesoamerican earthen architecture tradition arisen. It concerns thousands of sites made of raw earth: in the highlands earthen buildings exist alongside stone architecture, and often have a stone and stucco finish, while in the lowlands they are completely made of earth, with earthen facings, exceptionally lime-coated. The lowland sites span from the central part of the State of Veracruz in Mexico, across the Isthmus to the Pacific coast of Central America. These sites have always been known through their formal layout of plazas limited by pyramids and platforms (and often ball-courts in the form of two parallel elongated mounds). Yet until recently, these buildings were considered to be simple mounds of earth supporting rather primitive wattle-and-daub structures with palm-thatch roofs, a preconception based on their formal similarity with the long-known Mississippian mounds showing huge sequences of fills and on the adverse conditions of the humid tropical environment. Over the last 30 years, excavations in several sites have begun to show that these mounds are more than simple heaps of earthen fill, but are instead formal buildings, closely paralleling the better known stone architecture, and often their predecessors. To achieve this, special construction techniques were developed in order to make these buildings resistant to the environment. The sociopolitical context in which this expertise came about is the topic of this paper.

Antecedents

The oldest typically Mesoamerican buildings excavated up to now were made of raw earth: Paso de la Amada's ball-court and residence in Chiapas, from about 1600 BC (uncalibrated radiocarbon years, as are all dates henceforward) (Hill and Clark 2001), the sunken patio at San Lorenzo in southern Veracruz from about 1000 BC (Cyphers *et al.* 2006), and pyramid-plaza layouts at La Venta and other sites along the Grijalva basin between 800-400 BC (Gillespie 2008, Love *et al.* 2005) (Figure 1); all of these sites were excavated through trenches, sometimes enlarged in extensive excavations, but always reburied. The lowland sites belong to the greater isthmian area that is the seat of Mesoamerica's earliest complex societies, with the appearance of ceramic assemblages, together with ball-courts, cacao drinking, and a preference for jadeite as a sumptuary good. By 1200-900 BC, the Olmec center of San Lorenzo is at the apex of a tiered settlement pattern, its elite organizing the 1.3 million cubic

FIGURE 1. MAP WITH MAJOR EARTHEN ARCHITECTURE SITES CITED IN THE TEXT
(CONTOUR MAP BASED ON INEGI 1992 1:4,000,000 MAP OF MEXICO.

meter modification of the hill on which it sits, building palaces, bringing in tons of basalt stones for major sculpture programs, receiving long-distance goods (obsidian, jadeite, mica), producing food surpluses using recessional agriculture, and storing products like bitumen and ilmenite blocks, and exporting an ideological discourse set in a particular style to much of Mesoamerica, establishing the first 'horizon' (Cyphers et al. 2010: 134, Cyphers and Di Castro 1996, Wendt and Cyphers 2008). Although it is still a matter of controversy, the Olmec may have reached an early state level of integration, probably the first in Mesoamerica (see Pool 2007: 20-26 for an updated discussion). This is significant for our paper, because it shows that the origin of this early monumental earthen architecture tradition is part of the achievements of complex societies (*versus* Flannery and Marcus 2000). Although some constructive techniques of this culture are described, such as the use of bentonite clay blocks for floors, some with asphalt waterproofing, and thick earthen walls (Cyphers 1996, 1997: 99-102), the structure of the platform fills and the detailed evidence of different types of wall (adobe, cob, mud slurry or rammed earth?) and of roofing are still unpublished.

In these circumstances, the excavations at La Joya, on the central Gulf coast, that started as a salvage operation in a site heavily damaged by modern brick-making, provided the opportunity to record the stratigraphy of a very long building sequence and to carry out extensive excavations of complete buildings, retrieving different types of construction offerings and obtaining samples of fills, adobes from walls, roofing fragments, and facings of walls and floors. These data allowed understanding the variety and originality of the building techniques, the logic of the subsequent construction programs, the building layouts and functions, and the mineralogical and chemical composition of the building materials. These could then be compared with the vernacular architecture of the same period, demonstrating not only the quantitative but also, and most importantly, the qualitative difference between monumental and domestic construction. The technological supremacy of the first can only be understood through the sponsoring of elites, combined with the political clout to motivate a major labour force and to acquire or produce high quality building materials.

The La Joya sequence

La Joya is located at the confluence of the Jamapa and Cotaxtla rivers, in the central part of the state of Veracruz along the Gulf coast of Mexico (Figure 1). The earliest evidence of human occupation dates to about 1200 BC, with Olmec style ceramics and figurines, but no in situ deposits were found, when surface strata were removed as fill layers in the first building stages. The earliest structure is the North Platform, dating to 400-200 BC. This was a large, enclosed residence erected on the lower slope of a paleodune emerging from the alluvial terraces (Figure 2a), the central part of the hill being used as gathering place for large groups of people, as inferred by series of large underground ovens for massive food production (Daneels 2008a). By ad 300, the North Platform had become a large platform with administrative, public, ritual and residential buildings of adobes with flat roofs, bordering a closed plaza dominated by a 4-staircase pyramid to the west, and possibly another monumental platform to the east; to the south the compound was enlarged with a monumental construction delimiting a now much larger plaza to the south and east; the fill material was obtained by digging an inverted U-shaped water reservoir system in the alluvial terrace and leveling of the paleodune top (Figure 2b).

Three reservoirs now delimited the area of major architecture, protecting it from flooding (draining excess water through a shallow overflow canal northwards), and forcing visitors to go around the site to enter through the south. They also function as reflecting ponds, creating the visual perception of the site floating in water, a concept common to the Mesoamerican world view where the earth is a monster (crocodile, turtle or some hybrid aquatic animal) floating in primordial waters (Figure 2c). By ad 700 the pyramid was enlarged to double its original height, the whole monumental area elevated 2 m above the surrounding alluvial terrace level, and a new plaza laid out, including a ball-court facing the pyramid's southern façade; the entrance to the site was now severely restricted, physically and visually, with the new plaza and the main plaza accessible only through narrow passages, and

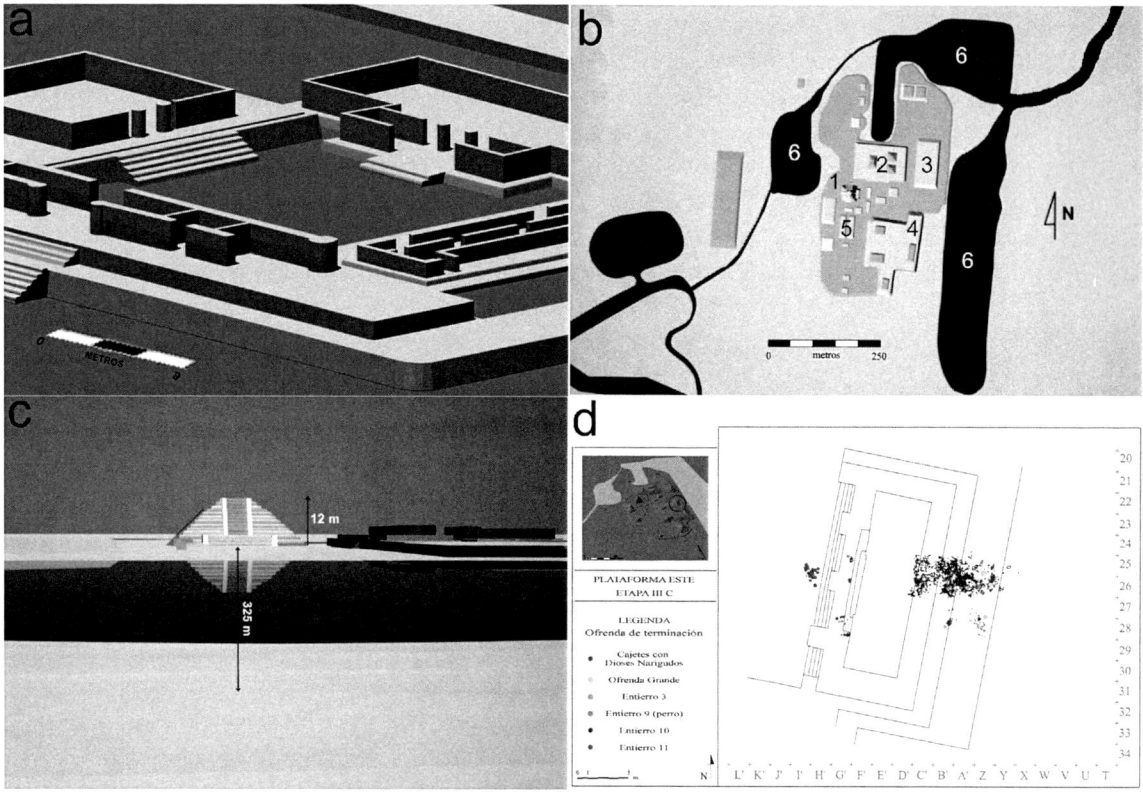

FIGURE 2. LA JOYA, 3D RECONSTRUCTIONS BASED ON ARCHAEOLOGICAL EVIDENCE: A. NORTH PLATFORM, FIRST BUILDING STAGE (BY GIOVANNA LIBEROTTI, IN 2011); B. GENERAL SITE MAP, FINAL BUILDING STAGE (1. PYRAMID, 2. NORTH PLATFORM, 3. NORTHEAST PLATFORM, 5. BALL COURT, 6. RESERVOIRS – DAVID PIÑA 2014); C. WATER RESERVOIR ACTING AS REFLECTING POND, VIEW FROM EAST DURING SECOND BUILDING STAGE (DAVID PIÑA 2014); D. LINE OF OFFERINGS IN FRONT AND AT THE BACK OF EAST PLATFORM'S THIRD BUILDING STAGE (BY GIOVANNA LIBEROTTI, IN 2011).

the main façades of the palace-platforms looking inwards (Figure 2b) (Daneels 2011). The site was abandoned by 1000 ad, and the Postclassic immigrant settlers that overtook the south-central region of Veracruz surrounded it without occupying the ruins (Daneels 1997, Stark 2008).

The building technology

The monumental quality of the buildings required developing special construction techniques to control the internal pressure of the fills, to protect large earthen surfaces from rain damage, to calculate load limits for large buildings with flat roofs and wide entrances (up to 3 m), and to control the rise of capillary humidity, skills today part of the expertise of architects and civil engineers. Controlling the internal pressure of amorphous fills is difficult, as they behave like natural strata stabilizing at a 27 degree slope, and even more difficult if the raw material consists of expansive clay, with a high expansion-contraction coefficient according to prevailing humidity conditions. The techniques used in other sites are adobe cells containing fills (in Teotihuacan, Cabrera 1991: 130-132) or complete adobe fills, as in La Venta, San José Mogote, Teotihuacan, San Andrés (Drucker *et al.* 1959: 90-92, Fernández and Hueda 2008: 564, Cabrera 1991: 133-134, Boggs 1943: 107).

In the case of La Joya, the system used starting with the first building stage was that of large squarish blocks of clay or clayey silt, several meters wide and about a meter high, laid out in a checkerboard pattern, with the intervening squares filled with sand. In this system, the clay blocks contained the sand, and the sand blocks impeded the expansion of the clay; it had the added advantage (compared to the adobe cells or fills previously described) of allowing the circulation of humidity both from rain or groundwater through the connecting sand squares, from the underlying soil surface level, without affecting the stability of the fill; the rain damage was checked by keeping all surfaces at a minimum slope and leading runoff from rooftops and plazas towards subsurface drainages made of fitted conical terracotta tubes that discharged in the reservoirs, which themselves represented a huge hydraulic system of flood protection against the seasonal rise in the river levels (Daneels and Guerrero 2011). The calculations for the slopes, the loads, and the spans were obviously derived after years of trial and error, but by the time La Joya was built evidently this knowledge was formalized, as no obvious correction measures were identified in existing buildings, and during remodeling new drainage systems were cut through existing buildings at optimum angles and slopes with a minimum of excavation.

The construction skills would nevertheless have been insufficient for the buildings to survive in the tropical lowlands had the building materials not been improved before using. The petrographic and mineralogical analysis of the construction samples at La Joya had shown the standard to low quality of the materials (Daneels and Guerrero 2011); particularly surprising was the proportion of clays and silts used in the adobes and facings, higher than the recommended in modern construction (Hall *et al*. 2013), especially in view of the expansive properties of the local clays and the strong variation in seasonal humidity. The chemical analyses were carried out expecting to find a clay stabilizing substance derived from plants used in vernacular earthen architecture, but the results showed the presence of a petroleum derivative (Kita *et al*. in press). As asphaltic emulsions are commonly used today to stabilize earth (Hall *et al*. 2013), we infer that this substance was part of the mud-mix preparation. Near La Joya were petroleum seeps, at less than 30 km upriver, along a geological fracture line crossed by the main rivers, and there is local evidence that the asphaltic fraction of crude was collected and thermally processed for waterproofing jars and painting figurines (Kita *et al*. in press).

The presence of the petroleum derivative in the construction samples (albeit without asphalt) implies an extra labour input, as the seeps are two day's walk away (one up, one back), and the product has to be either gathered in a special way to avoid the asphaltic component or has to be processed specially to separate and remove this heavy fraction. The petroleum derivative then has to be mixed thoroughly with the mud mix and the chopped grasses to prepare either adobes or facings. The finely chopped grasses, which compose up to 30-40% of these mixes and are important to add mechanical strength to the building material, also represent the result of a process so far not well understood; if obtained through cutting, this could only have been done with obsidian blades, representing a staggering amount of work in view of the volume of adobes and facings that reach into thousands of cubic meters in any one building stage at the site. In view of this evidence, simply preparing adequate mud-mixes for building required large amounts of man-hours.

Vernacular architecture, on the other hand, required none of this knowledge or complicated labour input. The basal platforms on which housing was erected, to avoid flooding problems, were low and had natural sloping sides, requiring no internal pressure control, stability being probably increased by allowing low vegetation to grow on the surface (grasses or possibly horticultural plants). When necessary in marshy terrain, capillary humidity was controlled by a damp-proof course of readily available insulating materials laid out under the floor area (layers of shells, sherds, jar necks, clay balls..., see Pérez 2002). The houses were of wattle and daub with gabled palm thatched roofs, lightweight, with wooden structural elements, with no need for subsurface drainage (neither adobes nor tubes have been found in such mounds).

Space sacrality and circulation

Another clear qualitative and quantitative difference exists between vernacular and monumental earthen architecture in the perception of space: how it is circumscribed and sacralized. Most residential, administrative, or ritual buildings in the south-central Veracruz area, where La Joya is situated, present evidence of consecration offerings (Fig. 2d). In the vernacular, even modest house mounds in small hamlets, readily accessible from most directions, will have offerings placed under the residence's floor; these will be small scale, both in quantity and contents, consisting of a few ceramic vessels and figurines (Daneels 2008b: examples of Plaza de Toros and Ixcoalco, within the study area – see Fig. 1). In major buildings of low ranking centers, the contents is similar but the quantity is increased to hundreds of vessels and figurines (Conchal Norte – Pérez 2002, La Campana – Jiménez and Bracamontes 2000, within the study area – see Fig. 1). Such small centers have open layouts, either 3 or 4 buildings around a plaza or a residential platform of considerable size; on the other hand, medium and high-ranking centers have closed layouts, delimited by reservoirs and constructions (Daneels 2008a). Though the offerings continue to be mainly ceramics and figurines in large quantities (hundreds, reaching into thousands), they are often complemented with human sacrificial remains (Las Puertas – Guerrero 2005, within the study area, Faisán – Hangert 1958, Zapotal – Torres 2004, Cerro de las Mesas – Drucker 1943 – see Fig. 1). These are not to be confused with normal burials: among the more than 80 individuals excavated in La Joya, only one is clearly a funerary deposit: an adult male in a large vessel, with sumptuous grave goods (Daneels and Ruvalcaba 2012); the rest are complete individuals or parts of them (heads, legs, arms, torsos) placed in the same stratigraphic deposit as the terracotta elements, in caches aligned with the construction. Such offerings are placed variously depending on the building: in corners in the North Platform, in the front or the back of the structure along its main axis in the East Platform, under the staircase balustrades in the Pyramid, or bracketing the main façade in the altar on the side of the pyramid (so far none have been placed in the geometric centers of the buildings) (Fig. 2d). The offerings thus show a pattern of contents that differentiates high ranking centers through the presence of sometimes abundant human sacrifice, a feature that can be linked to the power over life and death wielded by institutionalized governments.

Conclusion

Drawing mainly from the abundant recent data obtained in La Joya, but also from more scattered evidence from older publications, technical reports, and theses from the sout-central region of Veracruz, I have assessed the context in which a formal, monumental, earthen architecture arises and develops, particularly in the humid tropical lowlands where such architecture has only recently been identified as a formal tradition. The programmed layout and the calculi required to achieve the monumentality are evidence that – as we would put it today – architects and engineers were active in state-sponsored building programs. Central planning and authority are also implied by the labour input required to obtain and manufacture high quality building materials, as well as to carry out the monumental constructions and maintain them. In the social and ideological realm, a difference is also patent between low and high ranking centers (medium and high) in the closed architectural layouts and the presence of human sacrifice representing power over life and death. These data allow positing a close association between power (political) and the technology of monumental architecture. When the power base collapses in south-central Veracruz, and in the Postclassic period the cultural patterns are replaced by nahua highland norms (with stone and stucco architecture), the technology of monumental earthen architecture is lost, there being no memory of it in the vernacular architecture that did survive, as the latter was always distinct from the monumental architectural tradition.

Acknowledgements

The archaeological data presented in this article were obtained during several field seasons of the project 'Exploraciones en el Centro de Veracruz', of the Institute of Anthropological Research of the National Autonomous University of Mexico (UNAM), with the permission of the Mexican Council of Archaeology of the Instituto Nacional de Antropología e Historia (INAH), funds being provided by grants IN305503 (2004-2006), IN405009 (2009-2011) and IN300812 (2012-2014) of the Programa de Apoyo a Proyectos de Investigación e Innovación Tecnológica of the Dirección

General de Asuntos del Personal Académico (DGAPA) of the UNAM. Giovanna Liberotti and David Piña elaborated the 3D reconstructions based of the archaeological evidence recovered at the site of La Joya, the first as part of a postdoctoral grant of the Sapienza University of Rome, the latter as part of his MA thesis (Piña 2014), supported with an UNAM postgraduate grant.

Bibliography

Boggs, S. H. 1943. Notas sobre las excavaciones en la Hacienda 'San Andrés', Departamento de La Libertad. Tzunpame Año III, no. I, p. 104-126.

Cabrera-Castro, R. 1991. Los sistemas de relleno en algunas construcciones teotihuacanas. In Cabrera-Castro, R.; Rodríguez-García, I.; Morelos-García, N., coords. – Teotihuacan 1980-1982. Nuevas Interpretaciones. Mexico City: Instituto de Antropología e Historia, p. 113-143. (Colección Científica 227).

Cyphers, A. 1996. *Reconstructing Olmec Life* at San Lorenzo. In Benson E. P.; de la Fuente, B., eds., Olmec Art of Ancient Mexico. Washington D.C.: National Gallery of Art, p. 61-71.

Cyphers, A. 1997. La arquitectura olmeca en San Lorenzo Tenochtitlan. In Cyphers, A., ed., Población, subsistencia y Medio Ambiente en San Lorenzo Tenochtitlan. Mexico City: Instituto de Investigaciones Antropológicas, Universidad Nacional Autónoma de México, p. 91-118.

Cyphers, A.; Di Castro, A. 1996. Los artefactos multiperforados de ilmenita en San Lorenzo. Arqueología 16, p. 3-14.

Cyphers, A.; Hernández-Portilla, A.; Varela-Gómez, M.; Gregor-López, L. 2006. Cosmological and Sociopolitical Synergy in Preclassic Architectural Complexes. In Lucero, L. J.; Fash, B. W., eds., Precolumbian Water Management, Ideology, Ritual and Power. Tucson: University of Arizona Press, p. 17-32.

Cyphers, A.; Murtha, T.; Borstein, J.; Zurita-Noguera, J.; Lunagómez, R.; Symonds, S.; Jiménez, G.; Ortiz, M. A.; Figueroa, J. M. 2010. Arqueología digital en la primera capital olmeca, San Lorenzo. Thule. Rivista italiana di studi americanistici 22/23-24/25 (aprile/ottobre 2007-2008), p. 121-144.

Daneels, A. 1997. Settlement History in the Lower Cotaxtla Basin. In Stark, B. L.; Arnold, P. J., eds., Olmec to Aztec. Settlement Patterns in the Ancient Gulf Lowlands. Tucson: The University of Arizona Press, p. 206-252.

Daneels, A. 2008a. Monumental Earthen Architecture at La Joya, Veracruz, Mexico. Crystal River: Foundation for the Advancement of Mesoamerican Studies. [consult. 30 Jan. 2015]. Available at URL http://www.famsi.org/reports/07021.

Daneels, A. 2008b. Medellín Zenil y los Dioses Nariguados. Revista Contrapunto 7, Dossier Medellín Zenil, p. 52-74.

Daneels, A. 2011. Arquitectura cívico-ceremonial de tierra en la Costa del Golfo: el sitio de La Joya y el urbanismo del periodo Clásico. In Robles García, N. M.; Rivera-Guzmán, A. I., eds, Monte Albán en la encrucijada regional y disciplinaria. Memoria de la Quinta Mesa Redonda de Monte Albán. Mexico City: Instituto Nacional de Antropología e Historia, p. 445-478.

Daneels, A.; Guerrero-Baca, L. F. 2011. Millenary Earthen Architecture in the Tropical Lowlands of Mexico. APT Bulletin (Association for Preservation Technology) 42 (1), p. 11-18.

Daneels, A.; Ruvalcaba, J. L. 2012. Cuentas de piedra verde en una residencia Clásica del Centro de Veracruz, In Walburga W.; Guzzi, G., coords. – *El jade y otras piedras verdes: perspectivas interdisciplinarias e interculturales.* Mexico City: Instituto Nacional de Antropología e Historia-CONACULTA, p. 81-114.

Drucker, P. 1943. Ceramic Stratigraphy at *Cerro* de las *Mesas*, Veracruz, Mexico. Bureau of American Ethnology Bulletin 141. Washington, D.C.: Smithsonian Institution.

Drucker, P.; Heizer, R. F.; Squier, R. J. 1959. Excavations at La Venta, Tabasco, 1955. Bureau of American Ethnology Bulletin 170. Washington, D.C.: Smithsonian Institution. viii+97 p.

Fernández-Dávila, E.; Hueda-Tanabe, Y. 2008. San José Mogote, Oaxaca: una síntesis de permanencia histórica en proceso de extinción. In Uriarte, M. T.; González-Lauck, R., eds., Olmeca: balance y perspectivas: memoria de la primera mesa redonda. Mexico City: Universidad Nacional Autónoma de México, Instituto de Investigaciones Estéticas, Dirección General de Publicaciones y Fomento Editorial: Instituto Nacional de Antropología e Historia, Consejo Nacional para la Cultura y las Artes, New World Archaeological Foundation, Brigham Young University, p. 559-584.

FLANNERY, K.; MARCUS, J. 2000. Formative Mexican Chiefdoms and the Myth of the '*Mother* Culture'. Journal of Anthropological Archaeology 19, p. 1-37.

GILLESPIE, S. 2008. The Architectural History of La Venta Complex A: A Reconstruction Based on the 1955 Field Records. Crystal River: Foundation for the Advancement of Mesoamerican Studies. [Consult. March 1, 2015]. Available at http://www.famsi.org/reports/070254.

GUERRERO ANDRADE, M. 2005. Sitio arqueológico Las Puertas: excavación en arquitectura de tierra: un edificio construido en terracota. Tesis de Licenciatura en Arqueología. México City: Escuela Nacional de Antropología e Historia.

HALL, M. R.; NAJIM, K. B.; KEIKAHAEI, P. 2012. Soil stabilization and earth construction: materials, properties and techniques. In M. R. Hall; Linsdsay R.; Krayenhoff, M., eds., Modern Earth Buildings. Materials, engineering, construction and applications. Cambridge: Woodhead, p. 222-255.

HANGERT, W. 1958. Informe sobre el edificio no. 1 de El Faisán. La Palabra y el Hombre 7, p. 267-274.

HILL, W.; CLARK, J. E. 2001. Sports, Gambling, and Government: America's First Social Compact? American Anthropologist 103 (2), p. 331-345.

INEGI 1992. Map of Mexico, scale 1:4,000,000. Mexico City: Instituto Nacional de Estadística, Geografía e Informática.

JIMÉNEZ-PÉREZ, J.; BRACAMONTES-CRUZ, A. 2000. Estudio Arqueológico del Montículo de La Campana del Clásico Temprano, con arquitectura de barro cocido y Hallazgos asociados, en Jamapa en el Estado de Veracruz. México. Graduate thesis [licenciatura] in Archaeology. Mexico City: Escuela Nacional de Antropología e Historia.

KITA, Y.; DANEELS, A.; ROMO DE VIVAR, A. 2015. Uso de fracción ligera de crudo como estabilizante de tierra. In M. C. Achig Balarezo (coord.) Tierra, Sociedad, Comunidad. 15° Seminario Internacional de Arquitectura y Construcción con Tierra. Cuenca: Universidad de Cuenca, p. 103-111.

KITA, Y.; DANEELS, A.; ROMO DE VIVAR, A. (in press). Redeeming petroleum products for earthen architecture conservation, International Journal of Architectural Heritage.

LOVE, M.; CASTILLO-VALDÉZ, D.; UGARTE, R.; DAMIATA, B.; STEINBERG, J. 2005. Investigaciones Arqueológicas en el Montículo 1 de La Blanca, Costa Sur de Guatemala. In Laporte, J. P.; Arroyo, B.; Mejía, H. E., eds., XVIII Simposio de Investigaciones Arqueológicas en Guatemala. Guatemala City: Ministerio de Cultura y Deportes, Instituto de Antropología e Historia, Asociación Tikal, Foundation for the Advancement of Mesoamerican Studies, Inc., p. 959-969.

PÉREZ-BLAS, D. 2002. Conchal Norte: representación singular del desarrollo regional en la cuenca baja del río Cotaxtla a fines del periodo Clásico. Graduate thesis [licenciatura] in Archaeology. México City: Escuela Nacional de Antropología e Historia.

PIÑA-MARTÍNEZ, A. D. 2014. Los espacios arquitectónicos como reflejo del orden social', M. A. in Estudios Mesoamericanos, Mexico City: National Autonomous University of Mexico.

POOL, C. A. 2007. Olmec Archaeology and Early Mesoamerica. Cambridge: Cambridge University Press. 370 p.

STARK, B. L. 2008. Archaeology and Ethnicity in Postclassic Mesoamerica. In Berdan, F. F.; Chance, J. K.; Sandstrom, A.; Stark, B. L.; Taggart, J.; Umberger, E., eds., *Ethnic Identity in Nahua Mesoamerica: The View from Archaeology, Art History, Ethnohistory, and Contemporary Ethnography*. Salt Lake City: University of Utah Press, p. 38-63.

TORRES, M. 2004. Los entierros múltiples en la zona arqueológica de El Zapotal, Veracruz. In Lira-López, Y.; Serrano-Sánchez, C., eds., Prácticas funerarias en la Costa del Golfo de México. México City: Instituto de Antropología de la Universidad veracruzana, Instituto de Investigaciones Antropológicas de la Universidad Nacional Autónoma de México, Asociación Mexicana de Antropología Biológica, p. 203-212.

WENDT, C.; CYPHERS, A. 2008. How the Olmec Used Bitumen in Ancient Mesoamerica. Journal of Anthropological Archaeology 27(2), p. 175-191.

Activity areas in two ceremonial centers of the Southern Brazilian Highlands: relations between architecture and function

Jonas Gregorio DE SOUZA
Department of Archaeology, Centre for the Archaeology of the Americas,
University of Exeter (UK), 309 Laver Building, North Park Road, Exeter, EX4 4QE, UK
jonas.gregorio@yahoo.com.br

Abstract

In this article I present the analysis of the features and artefact assemblages of two mound and enclosure sites of the Southern Brazilian Highlands. Both exhibit rectangular annexes in their architecture, as well as a large quantity of lithics, which differentiates them from other sites of the same category. I suggest that the architectural complexity and activity areas evidenced in the sites point to a greater elaboration in mortuary ritual associated with greater architectural complexity in late periods. These distinctions may be related to the emergence of complex chiefdoms, as was reported for the Kaingang in the 19th century.

Keywords: *Southern Brazilian Highlands, Taquara/Itararé Tradition, enclosures, emergent complexity*

Résumé

Aires d'activités dans deux centres cérémoniels du Haut Plateau Méridional du Brésil: relations entre architecture et fonction

Dans cet article, je présente l"analyse des structures et des ensembles d'artefacts de deux sites de monticules et enceintes du Plateau du Sud du Brésil. Les deux sites présentent des annexes rectangulaires dans leur architecture, ainsi qu'une grande quantité de matériaux lithiques, qui les différencie des autres sites de la même catégorie. Je suggère que la complexité architecturale et les activités en évidence dans les sites pointent vers une plus grande élaboration dans le rituel funéraire associé à une plus grande complexité architecturale dans le période tardive. Ces distinctions peuvent être liés à l'émergence de chefferies complexes, comme a été rapporté pour les Kaingang au 19ème siècle.

Mots-clés: *Haut Plateau du Sud du Brésil, Tradition Taquara / Itararé, enceintes, complexité émergente*

Introduction

In this paper I explore the relationship between architectural variation in ceremonial earthworks and the different activities that took place in them, using as a case study the Taquara/Itararé Tradition of the Southern Brazilian Highlands. The Taquara/Itararé Tradition, which emerged in the Southern Brazilian Highlands around 2000 years before present, is characterised by small, thin ceramic vessels with a variety of plastic decorations, including incisions, punctuations and basketry impressions, as well as by pit house settlements and ceremonial earthworks such as mounds and enclosures (Schmitz, 1988; Noelli, 1999; Beber, 2004; Araujo, 2007). In fact, the ceremonial architecture of the Taquara/Itararé Tradition raised much interest since the earliest archaeological investigations in the Southern Brazilian Highlands (Menghin, 1957; Rohr, 1971; Ribeiro and Ribeiro, 1985). Burial mounds are found throughout the region, and it is attested that their construction persisted until the mid-twentieth century by the native peoples of the area, the Kaingang and Xokleng (Mabilde, 1897; Vasconcellos, 1912; Maniser, 1930; Métraux, 1946). This makes the Southern Brazilian Highlands one of the very few places in the Americas where mound building was an activity actually witnessed by chroniclers throughout the historical period.

In precolonial times, the ritual architecture of the Taquara/Itararé Tradition includes circular earthworks mostly enclosing burial mounds; these structures received several names in the literature,

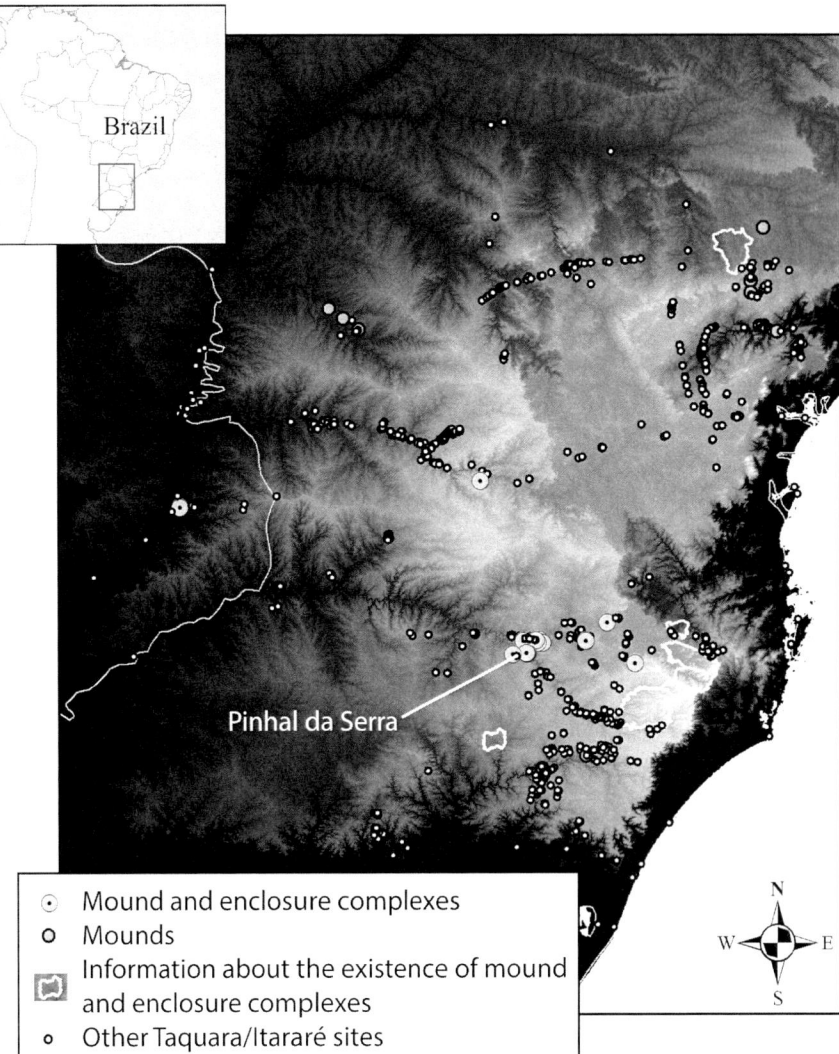

FIGURE 1. DISTRIBUTION OF MOUND AND ENCLOSURE COMPLEXES OF THE TAQUARA/ITARARÉ TRADITION AND INDICATION OF THE STUDY AREA (PINHAL DA SERRA).

such as 'ring structures' (Caldarelli, 2002) or 'enclosed areas' (Saldanha, 2005, 2008). Here, I will use the term 'mound and enclosure complex', as it is consolidated in the international literature (Iriarte *et al.*, 2013). This type of site is concentrated in the basins of the rivers Pelotas and Canoas (Rohr, 1971; Reis, 1980; Ribeiro and Ribeiro, 1985; Copé *et al.*, 2002; Saldanha 2005, 2008; De Masi, 2005, 2009; Müller, 2008; De Souza and Copé, 2010; Schmitz *et al.*, 2010; Corteletti, 2010, 2012; Iriarte *et al.*, 2013), but they can also be more sporadically found as far away as the province of Misiones, Argentina (Menghin, 1957; Iriarte *et al.*, 2008, 2010) as well as in the states of Paraná (Chmyz, 1968) and São Paulo (Chmyz *et al.*, 1968) (Figure 1). This type of earthwork emerges around AD 1000, coinciding with the greatest expansion of the Taquara/Itararé Tradition in the region (Iriarte and Behling, 2007; Corteletti, 2012, p. 197-201) (Figure 1).

Architectural variation in mound and enclosure complexes

A recent question in the study of these sites is the variation in their architecture (for instance, the dimensions of the earthworks, their layout, whether mounds are present or not) and how this relates to site function. In terms of size, a bimodal distribution is evident (De Masi, 2009, p. 110-111; De Souza and Copé, 2010; Iriarte *et al.*, 2013, p. 79-80). Small enclosures, with 15 to 30 m of diameter, usually are associated with burial mounds. They are often placed in pairs, with east-west alignments or variations of it, such as northeast-southwest (De Souza, 2007; Iriarte *et al.*, 2013, p. 83). In contrast, larger enclosures, with more than 60 m of diameter, often appear without mounds, only enclosing an open plaza. Some of them have entrance avenues (Menghin, 1957; Reis, 1980; Iriarte *et al.*, 2010, 2008).

To illustrate some hypotheses that have been suggested for the function of oversized enclosures, I will draw on examples taken from a study area in the municipality of Pinhal da Serra, state of Rio Grande do Sul, Brazil (Figure 1). This area is located in the core region of Taquara/Itararé occupation in the Highlands. The work in Pinhal da Serra started in the 1980s as part of a commercial archaeology project which persisted until 2009 (Ribeiro and Ribeiro, 1985; Copé *et al.*, 2002; De Souza and Copé, 2010). Later, a partnership between the University of Exeter, UK, and the Federal University of Rio Grande do Sul, Brazil, was formed to continue the research in the area with funding by the National Geographic Society and the Wenner-Gren Foundation (Iriarte *et al.*, 2013). This long history of research revealed a dense distribution of pit house settlements and mound and enclosure complexes in the study area.

The differences between large and small enclosures can be exemplified with data from the site RS-PE-29 (Figure 2). The site contains enclosures with both categories of size. Structure 3 is a typical mound and enclosure complex, with a pair of enclosures 20 m in diameter, each surrounding a mound. The excavations in one of the mounds revealed two burials: a primary cremation, with the funeral pyre still in place, and a secondary burial (De Souza and Copé, 2010, p. 105-106). In contrast, Structure 1 is an oversized enclosure with 80 m of diameter and no apparent mounds. The stratigraphy of the earthwork exhibited two layers of dark and yellowish clays which are not found elsewhere in the site, and appear to be exogenous (De Souza and Copé, 2010, p. 103-105). The fact that the enclosure was built with sediments not found in its immediate surroundings attests

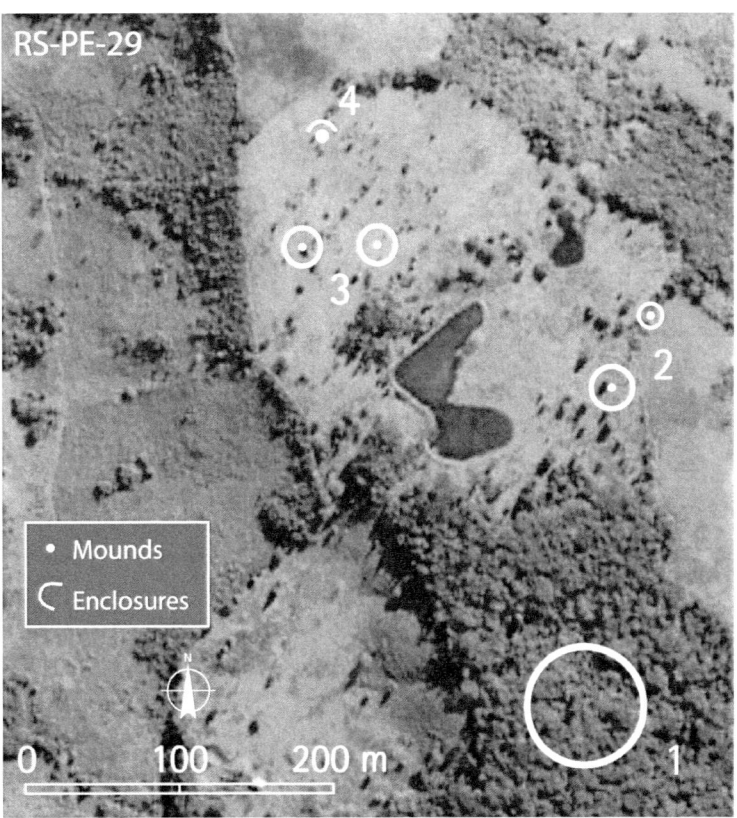

FIGURE 2. STRUCTURES OF THE SITE RS-PE-29.

a greater effort in its construction. Together with its large internal space, this is evidence that this structure was probably a large scale integrative facility (sensu Adler and Wilshusen, 1990) where a larger number of people congregated for rituals not involving burial. In contrast, small mound and enclosure complexes appear to be small scale facilities, serving as cemeteries for communities nearby (Saldanha, 2005, 2008; Copé, 2007; De Masi, 2009; De Souza and Copé, 2010; Iriarte *et al.*, 2013). In fact, pit house settlements are normally found less than 1 km from most mound and enclosure complexes (De Souza, 2012a).

Keyhole-shaped sites

However, there is more variability in the ritual architecture of the Taquara/Itararé Tradition than mere differences in size. The most atypical sites are the ones with rectangular annexes (Ribeiro and Ribeiro, 1985). The detailed topography of such sites revealed that the rectangular part is a late addition to an original circular architecture (Iriarte *et al.*, 2013, p. 84). Is it possible that this new architectural tradition is also correlated to different activities being performed at these sites? I will try to demonstrate that this is the case, with the analysis of artefact assemblages and features from the only two sites in the study area that exhibit rectangular architecture, sites RS-PE-31 and Posto Fiscal (Figure 3).

Unlike most of the mound and enclosure complexes, where few artefacts can be found apart from burials and votive pottery (Copé *et al.*, 2002, p. 130-131; DeMasi, 2005, p. 223-247; Müller, 2008, p. 40-52; De Souza and Copé, 2010, p. 105-106; Saldanha, 2005, p. 85-92), the architecturally complex sites with keyhole shapes and many mounds are characterised by a great concentration of artefacts and features.

The site RS-PE-31 consists of a circular enclosure 40 m in diameter around a central mound. A smaller enclosure, 20 m in diameter, and a rectangular earthwork trapezoidal in shape, 30 by 15 m, are attached to it (Figure 3a). The excavations in an area between the enclosures revealed a great concentration of quartz and flint flakes associated with a cluster of basalt rocks and charcoal, possibly a hearth (De Souza, 2012a).

The main structure of the site Posto Fiscal consists of a circular enclosure 30 m in diameter attached to a rectangular enclosure also 30 m wide. This keyhole-shaped structure surrounds three mounds, aligned east-west (Figure 3b). Close to this structure, one finds two smaller enclosures, each 20 m

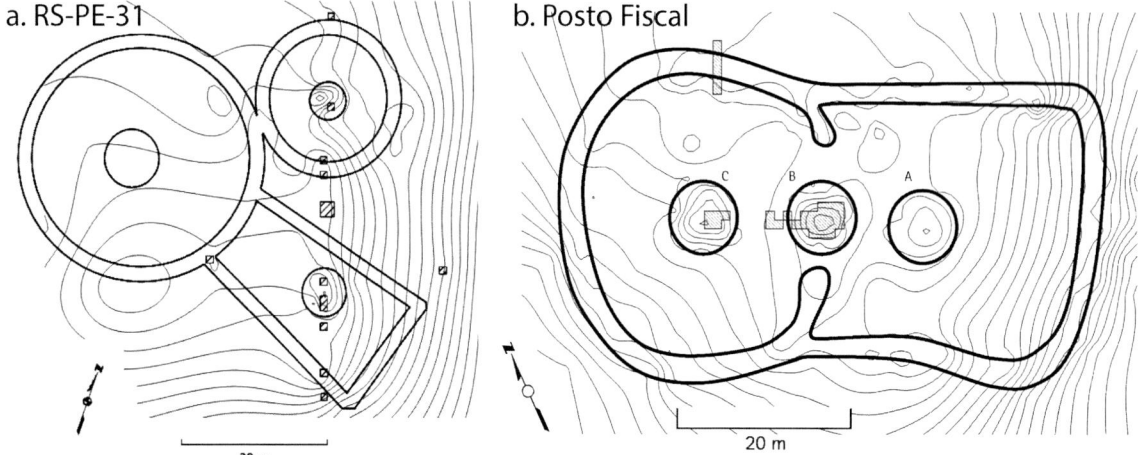

FIGURE 3. SITES RS-PE-31 (A) AND POSTO FISCAL (B). ONLY THE MAIN STRUCTURE OF THE LAST IS SHOWN.

in diameter. I will focus the discussion on the excavation of the central mound, called mound B, and its surroundings.

About 30 cm in depth, a lens of burnt earth of about 1 m² was found (Figure 4a). It was associated with small, calcinated bones. 20 cm beneath this layer of burnt earth, and in other areas at the base of the mound, discrete clusters of stones were found (Figure 4b), resembling stone ovens known elsewhere in the Taquara/Itararé Tradition (Iriarte *et al.*, 2008, 2010; De Masi, 2005, 2009). Beneath the mound, starting at 60 cm of depth, three elongated pits were evidenced, possibly graves (Figure 4c). They are in average 175 cm long, and between 30 and 40 cm deep. One of them contained a complete vessel, as well as small fragments of calcinated bone. Finally, an exceptional amount of lithics and ceramics were located (De Souza, 2012a, p. 52-60; Iriarte *et al.*, 2013, p. 84-87).

The following dates were obtained: charcoal from the bank of the circular enclosure was dated 1070 ±40 BP, Cal. AD 890-1020 (Beta-303594), whereas charcoal recovered from the burnt earth lens in mound B was dated 330±30 BP, Cal. AD 1480-1640 (Beta-304479) (Iriarte *et al.*, 2013, p. 82). Therefore, considering the calibrated dates, the circular earthwork precedes in at least 400 years the elaboration of the earthworks by the addition of mound B and, by extension, the rectangular annex.

Artefact assemblages of keyhole-shaped sites

The lithic artefact assemblage (n = 166) of the site RS-PE-31 is almost completely composed by débitage, i.e. flakes, cores, and knapping residues (81%). Microflakes (smaller than 1 cm), for reasons that will be clear later, were considered a separate category, constituting 18% of the assemblage. Apart from that, only one biface thinning flake has been identified. In terms of raw materials, quartz accounts for 75% of the total, followed by basalt (17%). Nearly all of the artefacts are concentrated in a small unenclosed area, between the smaller circular enclosure and the rectangular enclosure.

Similarly, the assemblage (n = 1,214) of the site Posto Fiscal is mostly composed by débitage (93%). There is a small number of microflakes (5%), biface thinning flakes (0.5%), and bifacial and unifacial instruments (1%), as well as a pestle fragment and a pebble used as a percussor. Unlike RS-PE-31, where quartz dominates the assemblage, in Posto Fiscal flint is the preferred raw material (43%), followed by basalt (33%). The sites are very close to each other, separated by approximately 1 km, and therefore the choice for different raw materials is probably cultural.

In terms of the vertical distribution of the artefacts, in mound B most of it is concentrated at the same level as the stone clusters, that is, at the base of the mound, between 35 and 40 cm of depth (Figure 4c). In terms of horizontal distribution, the greatest quantity of lithics comes from the area between mounds B and C; however, when we consider only the flakes with macroscopic use wear, it is possible to notice that they are concentrated beneath mound B, coinciding with the stone clusters (De Souza, 2012a, b). The evidence, therefore, points to an extensive activity area which preceded the construction of mound B. These activities were superimposed to the pits beneath the mound. These pits, as mentioned above, could be funerary in nature, as suggested by the scarce presence of calcinated bones; however, given the almost complete absence of remains, it is probable, as suggested by Iriarte *et al.* (2013), that they were temporary graves. That would point to a complex and multi-staged funerary ritual occurring at the site. The typical mound and enclosure complexes have almost no artefacts apart from eventual votive ceramics in the mounds (Copé *et al.*, 2002, p. 130-131; De Masi, 2005, p. 223-247; Müller, 2008, p. 40-52; De Souza and Copé, 2010, p. 105-106; Saldanha, 2005, p. 85-92). In contrast, the two sites analysed here exhibit dense concentrations of lithics, suggesting that a greater diversity of activities were carried out in these places.

To ascertain the nature of these activities, I compared the assemblages from sites RS-PE-31 and Posto Fiscal with a domestic context, represented by the pit house settlement RS-PE-41, located in the vicinity of the mound and enclosure complexes (Copé, 2008). The composition of the lithic assemblage of the domestic site RS-PE-41 was found to be very similar to that of Posto Fiscal

FIGURE 4. FEATURES IN MOUND B, SITE POSTO FISCAL: (A) LENS OF BURNT EARTH; (B) STONE CLUSTERS; (C) SCHEMATIC STRATIGRAPHIC DISTRIBUTION OF THE FEATURES IN THE MOUND.

(De Souza, 2012b). If we assume that the activities in the domestic context include processing and consumption of food, as well as the manufacturing and maintenance of tools, then the same activities might have been present in Posto Fiscal, though with different meanings given its ritual context. The site RS-PE-31 exhibits noticeable differences, mostly due to the abundance of quartz microflakes. Odell (1994), comparing the use wear in microblades from burial and domestic contexts in Middle Woodland sites of the Eastern United States, concludes that the microblades in burial sites were probably used for manufacturing items of perishable materials intended to be used in ceremonies or as funerary offerings (see also Carr, 2006c, p. 465-468). I believe that a similar possibility should be considered for the Taquara/Itararé context.

Discussion and conclusion

In summary, the sites RS-PE-31 and Posto Fiscal are unique in the study area due to their architectural characteristics, but also to the activities that probably took place in them. This is evidenced by the artefact assemblages and features, especially in Posto Fiscal. As part of the settlement system of many early formative societies and chiefdoms, multiple cemeteries were in use for the burial of different segments of the society, and these cemeteries should vary in terms of dimensions, structure and content (Binford, 1971; O'Shea, 1984; Peebles and Kus, 1977; Carr, 2006a, p. 77-78, 2006b, p. 243). I believe the following evidences suggest that the sites RS-PE-31 and Posto Fiscal were reserved for the celebration of a specific class of ancestors, possibly from a high-status segment of the society:

1. Architecturally complex sites such as these are fewer in number than the typical mound and enclosure complexes (Binford, 1971; O'Shea, 1984; Peebles and Kus, 1977);
2. The complexity in their architecture points to a greater investment of energy in their construction (Tainter, 1978), in a similar way as has been argued for oversized enclosures with the presence

of exogenous sediments (De Souza and Copé, 2010, p. 103-105). However, it is important to observe that the dates from Posto Fiscal (Cal. AD 890-1640, see above) suggest that this energy investment happened in the long term, which makes this site a persistent monumental place (sensu Thompson and Pluckhahn, 2012);

3. The artefact assemblages from the two sites point to a greater diversity of activities performed in those cemeteries (Carr, 2006b, p. 246);
4. These activities could involve the manufacturing of ritual items to accompany the dead, pointing to a greater investment in the production of the funerary offerings (Odell, 1994; Carr, 2006c, 465-468);
5. The activities could also involve the preparation and consumption of food, resembling funerary feasts (Twiss, 2008; Hayden, 2009), which in fact were described in the Southern Brazilian Highlands during the 19th century as being a part of the funerals of paramount chiefs (Mabilde, 1897, p. 162-166).

I believe that a large, regional population might have congregated at these sites for the celebration of burials or post-burial rites of regional leaders. This would be the earliest correlate of the political organisation of the peoples of the Southern Brazilian Highlands described in historical times. In the 19th century, the Kaingang were organised in chiefdoms with two levels of hierarchy, divided in paramount and subordinate chiefs (Mabilde, 1899, p. 142; Fernandes, 2004, p. 102-103). In many early formative societies, the promotion of funerary feasts is a common strategy of early leaders for consolidating the power of their lineage, together with the construction of monuments to their ancestors (Earle, 1997; Bradley, 1998, p. 132-146; Vega-Centeno, 2007; Hayden, 2009, p. 37-38; Iriarte *et al.*, 2008, 2010).

Finally, if we consider the dates of the site Posto Fiscal, which demonstrate that the site became architecturally more complex at Cal. AD 1480-1640 (see above), we can conclude that the emergence of chiefdoms – which, as I explained in the previous paragraph, can be inferred from the appearance of a few very elaborate burials and post-burial rites in opposition to the majority of the funerary sites – could be a relatively recent phenomenon in the Southern Brazilian Highlands, perhaps immediately preceding or even contemporary with the arrival of Europeans in the region.

Bibliography

ADLER, M.; WILSHUSEN, R. 1990. Large-scale integrative facilities in tribal societies: cross-cultural and Southwestern U.S. examples. World Archaeology. 22:2, p. 133-146.

ARAUJO, A. G. M. 2007. A tradição cerâmica Itararé-Taquara: características, área de ocorrência e algumas hipóteses sobre a expansão dos grupos Jê no sudeste do Brasil. Revista de Arqueologia. São Paulo. 20, p. 9-38.

BEBER, M. V. 2004. O sistema de assentamento dos grupos ceramistas do planalto sul-brasileiro: o caso da Tradição Taquara/Itararé. PhD Dissertation. São Leopoldo: UNISINOS.

BINFORD, L. 1971. Mortuary practices: their study and their potential. American Antiquity. 36, p. 6-29.

BRADLEY, R. 1998. The significance of monuments on the shaping of human experience in Neolithic and Bronze Age Europe. London: Routledge.

CALDARELLI, S. B. 2002. Projeto de levantamento arqueológico na área de inundação e salvamento arqueológico no canteiro de obras da UHE Barra Grande, SC/RS. Relatório Final 1: Resultados dos trabalhos de campo. Florianópolis: Scientia Ambiental.

CARR, C. 2006a. Salient issues in the social and political organizations of northern Hopewellian peoples. In Carr, C.; Case, D. T. eds. Gathering Hopewell: society, ritual, and ritual interaction. New York: Springer, p. 73-118.

CARR, C. 2006b. The question of ranking in Havana Hopewellian societies. In Carr, C.; Case, D. T. eds. Gathering Hopewell: society, ritual, and ritual interaction. New York: Springer, p. 238-257.

CARR, C. 2006c. Scioto Hopewell ritual gatherings. In Carr, C.; Case, D. T. eds. Gathering Hopewell: society, ritual, and ritual interaction. New York: Springer, p. 463-479.

CHMYZ, I. 1968. Subsídios para o estudo arqueológico do Vale do Rio Iguaçu. Revista do CEPA. Curitiba. 1, p. 31-52.

CHMYZ, I.; PEROTA, C.; MUELLER, H. I.; ROCHA, M. L. F. 1968. Notas sobre a arqueologia do vale do rio Itararé. Revista do CEPA. Curitiba. 1, p. 7-23.

COPÉ, S. M. 2007. El uso de la arquitectura como artefacto en el estudio de paisajes aqueológicos del altiplano sur brasileño. Revista de Arqueología. Universidad del Mar del Plata. 2, p. 15-34.

COPÉ, S. M. 2008. Escavações arqueológicas em Pinhal da Serra, RS: atividades laboratoriais realizadas em 2006 e 2007. Porto Alegre: Núcleo de Pesquisas Arqueológicas da Universidade Federal do Rio Grande do Sul.

COPÉ, S. M.; SALDANHA, J. D. M.; CABRAL, M. P. 2002. Contribuições para a pré-história do planalto: estudo da variabilidade de sítios arqueológicos de Pinhal da Serra, RS. Pesquisas: Antropologia. São Leopoldo. 58, p. 121-139.

CORTELETTI, R. 2010. Atividades de campo e contextualização do Projeto Arqueológico Alto Canoas – PARACA: um estudo da presença proto-Jê no Planalto Catarinense. Cadernos do LEPAARQ. Pelotas. 7, p. 121-157.

CORTELETTI, R. 2012. Projeto Arqueológico Alto Canoas – PARACA: um estudo da presença proto-Jê no Planalto Catarinense. PhD Dissertation. Sao Paulo: Museu de Arqueologia e Etnologia da Universidade de São Paulo.

DE MASI, M. A. N. 2005. Relatório Final: Projeto de Salvamento Arqueológico Usina Hidrelétrica de Campos Novos. Tubarão: Unisul.

DE MASI, M. A. N. 2009. Centros cerimoniais do planalto meridional: uma análise intrasítio. Revista de Arqueologia. São Paulo. 22, p. 99-113.

DE SOUZA, J. G. 2007. Significados da morte: interpretando as estruturas funerárias de Pinhal da Serra (RS) e Anita Garibaldi (SC). In Anais do XIV Congresso da Sociedade de Arqueologia Brasileira (CD-ROM). Florianópolis: Sociedade de Arqueologia Brasileira.

DE SOUZA, J. G. 2012a. Paisagem ritual no planalto meridional brasileiro: complexos de aterros anelares e montículos funerários Jê do Sul em Pinhal da Serra, RS. Master's Thesis. São Paulo. Museu de Arqueologia e Etnologia da Universidade de São Paulo.

DE SOUZA, J. G. 2012b. Áreas de atividade em dois centros cerimoniais jê do sul: relações entre arquitetura e função. Revista de Arqueologia. São Paulo. 25:2, p. 120-138.

DE SOUZA, J. G.; COPÉ, S. M. 2010. Novas perspectivas sobre a arquitetura ritual do planalto meridional brasileiro: pesquisas recentes em Pinhal da Serra, RS. Revista de Arqueologia. São Paulo. 23:2, p. 98-111.

EARLE, T. 1997. How chiefs come to power: the political economy in prehistory. Stanford: Stanford University Press.

FERNANDES, R. C. 2004. Uma contribuição da antropologia política para a análise do faccionalismo kaingang. In Tommasino, K.; Mota, L. T.; Noelli, F. S. eds. Novas contribuições aos estudos interdisciplinares dos Kaingang. Londrina: EDUEL. 83-143 p.

HAYDEN, B. 2009. Funerals as feasts: why are they so important? Cambridge Archaeological Journal. 19:1, p. 29-52.

IRIARTE, J.; BEHLING, H. 2007. The expansion of Araucaria forest in the southern Brazilian highlands during the last 4000 years and its implications for the development of the Taquara/Itararé Tradition. Environmental Archaeology. 12:2, p. 115-127.

IRIARTE, J.; GILLAM, J. C.; MAROZZI, O. 2008. Monumental burials and memorial feasting: an example from the southern Brazilian highlands. Antiquity. 82:318, p. 947-961.

IRIARTE, J.; MAROZZI, O.; GILLAM, J. C. 2010. Monumentos funerarios y festejos rituales: complejos de recintos y montículos Taquara/Itararé en El Dorado, Misiones (Argentina). Arqueología Iberoamericana. 6, p. 25-38.

IRIARTE, J.; COPÉ, S. M.; FRADLEY, M.; LOCKHART, J.; GILLAM, C. 2013. Sacred landscapes of the southern Brazilian highlands: Understanding southern proto-Jê mound and enclosure complexes. Journal of Anthropological Archaeology. 32:1, p. 74-96.

MABILDE, P. A. B. 1897. Apontamentos sobre os indígenas selvagens da nação 'Coroados' que habitam os sertões do Rio Grande do Sul. Anuário do Estado do Rio Grande do Sul. Porto Alegre. 13, p. 145-167.

MABILDE, P. A. B. 1899. Apontamentos sobre os indígenas selvagens da nação 'Coroados' que habitam os sertões do Rio Grande do Sul. Anuário do Estado do Rio Grande do Sul. Porto Alegre. 15, p. 125-151.

MANISER, H. H. 1930. Les Kaingang de São Paulo.In Proceedings of the 23rd International Congress of Americanists.New York. p. 760-791.

MENGHIN, O. F. 1957. El poblamiento prehistórico de Misiones. Anales de Arqueología y Etnología. Buenos Aires. 12, p. 19-40.

MÉTRAUX, A. 1946. The Caingang. In Steward, J., ed. Handbook of South American Indians, Vol. 1: The Marginal Tribes. Washington D.C.: Government Printing Office, p. 445-475.

MÜLLER, L. M. 2008. Sobre índios e ossos: estudo de três sítios de estruturas anelares construídos para enterramento por populações que habitavam o vale do rio Pelotas no período pré-contato. Master's Thesis. Porto Alegre. PUCRS.

NOELLI, F. S. 1999. Repensando os rótulos e a história dos Jê no sul do Brasil a partir de uma interpretação interdisciplinar. Revista do Museu de Arqueologia e Etnologia. São Paulo. 3, p. 285-302.

ODELL, G. H. 1994. The role of stone bladelets in Middle Woodland society. American Antiquity. 59:1, p. 102-120.

O'SHEA, J. 1984. Mortuary Variability: An Archaeological Investigation. Orlando: Academic Press.

PEEBLES, C. S.; KUS, S. 1977. Some archaeological correlates of ranked societies. American Antiquity. 42, p. 421-448.

REIS, M. J. 1980. A problemática arqueológica das estruturas subterrâneas no planalto catarinense. Masther's Thesis. São Paulo: Universidade de São Paulo.

RIBEIRO, P. A. M.; RIBEIRO, C. T. 1985. Levantamentos arqueológicos no município de Esmeralda, RS, Brasil. Revista do Centro de Ensino e Pesquisas Arqueológicas. Santa Cruz. 12:14, p. 49-105.

ROHR, J. A. 1971. Os sítios arqueológicos do planalto catarinense, Brasil. Pesquisas: Antropologia. São Leopoldo. 24, p. 1-56.

SALDANHA, J. D. M. 2005. Paisagem, lugares e cultura material: uma arqueologia espacial nas terras altas do sul do Brasil. Master's Thesis. Porto Alegre: PUCRS.

SALDANHA, J. D. M. 2008. Paisagem e sepultamento nas Terras Altas do Sul do Brasil. Revista de Arqueologia. São Paulo. 21, p. 85-95.

SCHMITZ, P. I. 1988. As tradições ceramistas do planalto sul-brasileiro. Documentos. São Leopoldo. 2, p. 75-130.

SCHMITZ, P. I.; ARNT, F. V.; BEBER, M. V.; ROSA, A. O.; FARIAS, D. S. 2010. Casas subterrâneas no planalto de Santa Catarina: São José do Cerrito. Pesquisas: Antropologia. São Leopoldo. 68, p. 7-78.

TAINTER, J. A. 1978. Mortuary Practices and the Study of Prehistoric Social Systems. In Schiffer, M. B. ed. Advances in Archaeological Method and Theory, vol. 1. New York: Academic Press, p. 105-141.

THOMPSON, V. D.; PLUCKHAHN, T. J. 2012. Monumentalization and ritual landscape at Fort Center in the Lake Okeechobee basin of South Florida. Journal of Anthropological Archaeology. 31:1, p. 49-65.

TWISS, K. C. 2008. Transformations in an early agricultural society: Feasting in the Southern Levantine Pre-Pottery Neolithic. Journal of Anthropological Archaeology. 27, p. 418-442.

VASCONCELLOS, D. R. 1912. Botocudos. Revista da Sociedade de Geografia do Rio de Janeiro. Rio de Janeiro. 17, p. 19-22.

VEGA-CENTENO, R. 2007. Construction, labor organization, and feasting during the Late Archaic Period in the Central Andes. Journal of Anthropological Archaeology. 26, p. 150-171.

New data on the Neolithic ditches of the Tavoliere area (Apulia, Southern Italy)

Annamaria TUNZI
Superintendence for Archaeological Heritage of Puglia, Bari, Italy
annamaria.tunzi@beniculturali.it

Tania QUERO
Specialisation School in Archaeological Heritage, University of Venice, Udine, Trieste, Italy
taniaquero82@gmail.com

Abstract

This paper presents some data from the most recent studies conducted in the Tavoliere region (Apulia, Southern Italy). In 2013, the first complete excavation of a Neolithic single ditch was carried out at the Amendola Air Base (Foggia), the pits found at the bottom suggest that the ditch was also used as quarry for clay. Instead, in the high Tavoliere region near Troia district, we explored a village comprised of four enclosure ditches and other internal features, which could reveal a different settlement system from the coastal plain.

Key-words: *Hypogeal structures, Early Neolithic, excavations, settlement pattern*

Résumé

Nouvelles données sur les fossés néolithiques de la région de Tavolière (Pouilles, Italie du Sud)

On présente les données des plus récentes recherches dans le Tavoliere des Pouilles (Italie méridionale). En 2013, la première fouille intégrale d'un fossé néolithique a été réalisée dans l'aéroport militaire d'Amendola (Foggia). Les fosses au fond suggèrent une utilisation aussi comme carrière pour l'approvisionnement de l'argile. En plus, dans l'haute Tavoliere, chez Troia, on a conduit des recherches dans un village caractérisé par quatre fossés d'enceinte et d'autres structures internes. Il s'agirait d'une différente organisation d'un village sur la colline, loin de la côte.

Mots-clés: *Structures hypogées, Néolithique Ancien, fouilles, organisation du territoire*

Introduction

To date, there are at least one thousand Neolithic settlements in the Tavoliere area (Apulia, Southern Italy), assigned to different chronological periods. The first were located by J. Bradford, a R.A.F official who used aerial photographs for researching the territory during the Post-WWII period. After Bradford Italian scholars like Puglisi, Tiné, Jones, Cassano and Manfredini conducted important surveys and excavations. Since 2002, the British Academy 'The Tavoliere-Gargano Prehistory Project' is in progress, however the results are to be published. New investigations for the local 'Carta Archeologica' (archaeological survey map) and several rescue excavations are increasing the number of known settlements. The sites are located at a distance of at least 2 km from each other on the top of low rises (called 'coppe') and cut into Pleistocene alluvial terraces, above the modern alluvial valleys, in ecotonal locations (Skeates 2000, p. 157), at a distance of 1 km from the rivers.[1]

In these sites, enormous ditches up to 4m deep and over 5 m wide, are hypogeal structures excavated in the bedrock by means of calcareous picks or big pebbles (Cassano, Manfredini 2004, p. 476). Generally, they are bell-shaped and the sides and the base are either straight or hollow. Sometimes

---

[1] The Early Neolithic in this region, had a temperate climate, with an increase in rainfall in the following periods (Delano Smith, 1983, p. 19-21; Caldara *et al.*, 2004, p. 31-36). The sea level was at -15 m compared to the present and a coastal lagoon developed. The vegetation was rich and diversified, with mixed woods covering the higher areas.

there are wide and shallow steps carved into the rock and some stone walls that obstruct the inner space. At several places, it is possible to recognise a combination of large external enclosure ditches and internal C-compounds, which divide the internal spaces of the settlements. The ditches could extend between a range of few hundreds of m² to a few tens of ha.

The area encircled by the ditches was organised such that every part had its own function, which is evidenced by some floor remains, postholes, pits/wells and other small ditches. There could be a kind of hierarchy among these sites. These settlements have several short-lasting phases of occupation. The precise use of these hypogeal structures is still uncertain: they were probably used for draining marshy areas or alternatively for water collection (Brown 1995, p. 188-192; Radina, Sarti, 2002, p. 197-200), isolating cattle, fields and huts or to delimit the territory of a community (Cassano, Manfredini 1983, p. 196-197). They could also have a symbolic and ritual value (Brown 1995, p. 188-192), demarcating the known space from the unknown, domesticated places from the wilderness (note that these Neolithic groups practiced both agricultural and pastoral activities). Some burials took place at the bottom or in the walls of the ditches.

These constructions required a significant work organisation and involved several individuals.[2] The evident effort to construct them could confirm the success of some social groups to mobilise the community, reinforcing the membership and avoid conflicts (Brown 1991, p. 26). The circular shape of the villages could have also contained symbolically the demographic growth of the communities (Cassano, Manfredini 2004, p. 476).

The C-shaped ditches (or C-compounds), more frequent in recent contexts, have been traditionally associated with dwellings of single family groups or enclosures for the protection/isolation of cattle (Cassano, Manfredini 2004, p. 477-478). They are often placed within the enclosure ditches (rarely on the outside), having the entrance in the same direction (this can suggest the contemporaneity of these collective works). Their deep cavities could also host some burials, but their association with huts or other dwelling features is uncertain. Furthermore, according to Skeates (2000, p. 181) they were part of '[…] a dynamic process of construction and modification, excavation and deposition, occupation and abandonment' and they '[…] played an active role in forming and transforming social relations in the […] Neolithic of the Tavoliere'. In this discussion, the paper presents some data from the most recent research in this region.

The context of the Amendola Air Base (Foggia)

Between 2012 and 2013, the first complete excavation of a single-ditched enclosure was carried out at the Amendola Air Base (Foggia) (Tunzi, Quero, in press). First the archaeologists of ArcheoRes S.r.l. and then Andrea Monaco, Ramon Simonetti and Tania Quero conducted the excavations, under the scientific direction of the Superintendence for Archaeological Heritage of Puglia (Dr. Annamaria Tunzi).

The ditch lay on the top of a 'coppa' of 55-60 m of altitude above the Amendola Plain, near the Candelaro River (4 km) and the coast (Figure 1A). It is possible that this ditch corresponds to the one G. D. B. Jones identified through old aerial photographs in the 80's (Jones 1987, p. 95). He considered that the ditch was destroyed, in the time of the researches for his PhD., but in 2012, the excavators confirmed the presence of that ditch, damaged partially in two sectors by recent infrastructural works.

The ditch cuts the bedrock, a Holocene evaporitic carbonate layer (*crusta*) with Pleistocene sandy marine deposits at the bottom (Ciaranfi 1983, p. 209-214; Caldara *et al.*, 2004, p. 29-30). It is

---

[2] Brown (1991, p. 14-22) calculated that in the smaller sites 12-24 people were involved for up to 20,000 construction-hours. In the complex settlements 70-168 up to 600 people (in some cases over 1000) worked for 60,000-100,000 construction-hours. Analysing the settlements organisation along the Candelaro river, Monaco (2011, p. 74-79) calculated by models a population density of 11 individuals per kmq.

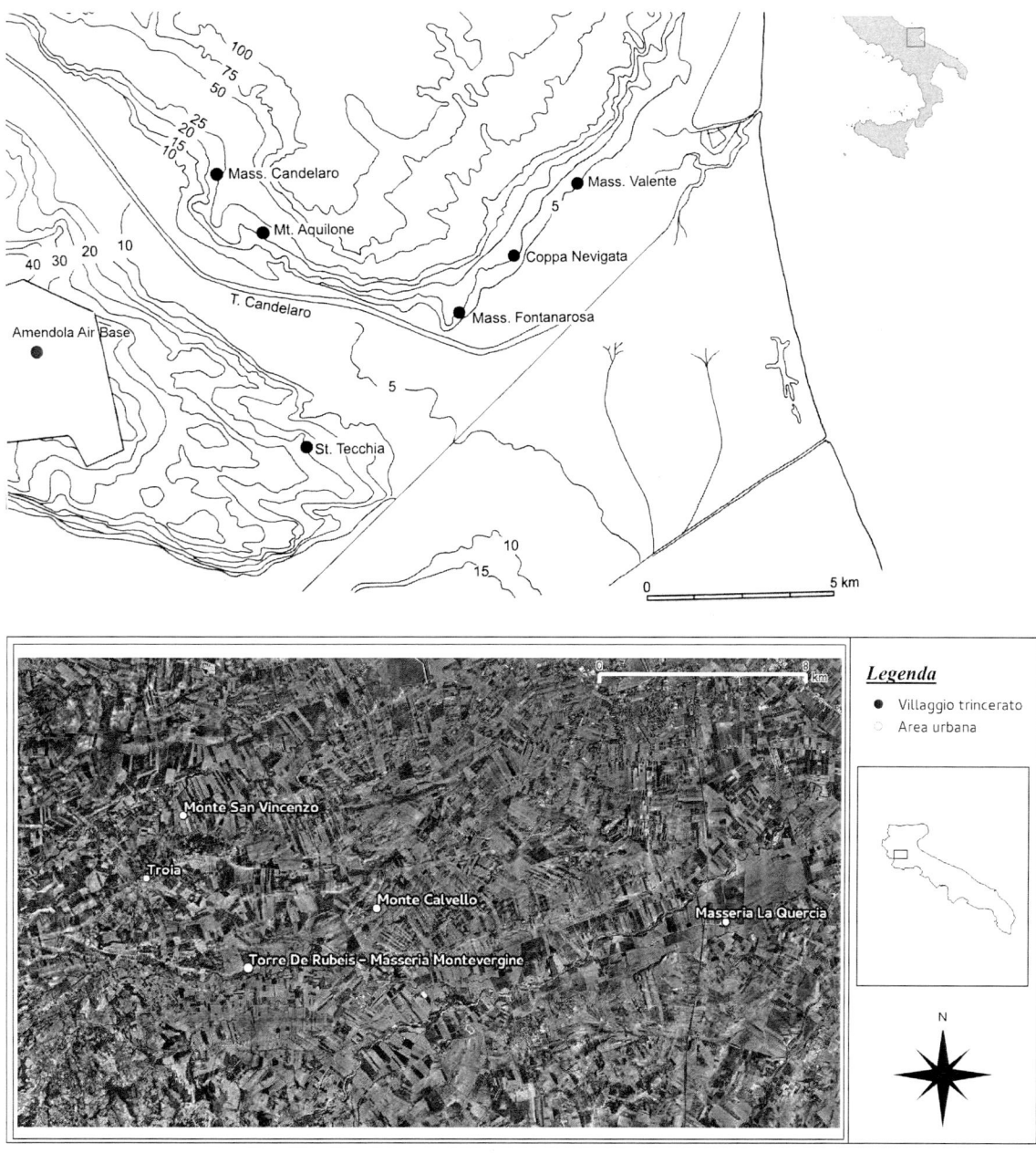

FIGURE 1. LOCATION OF THE SITES OF THE AMENDOLA AIR BASE (ABOVE)
AND MASSERIA MONTEVERGINE (BELOW).

elliptically-shaped, oriented E-W, covering an area of 8311 m^2; two passages, about 3 m wide, allowed entry into the inner area from the East and South (Figure 2).The average width of the ditch is about 3.80 m and the depth is about 1.90-2 m from the surface. The depth of the hypogeal structure circuit changes dramatically; the greater depth is in the southern sector, near one of the passages.

In general, loose and unordered sediments filled the structure: silt and clay soils could have several rock fragments and they were subjected to pedogenetic processes such as bioturbation and evapotranspiration. The walls displayed a variety of deep concavities and small holes due to water/wind erosion and faunal activities (burrowing organisms). At the sides and at the bottom of the ditch, there were more or less shallow holes (Figure 3), 0.55-0.90 m deep and round or rectangular in shape. They could be the result of reclaims and raw material extractions (clay for example) or water

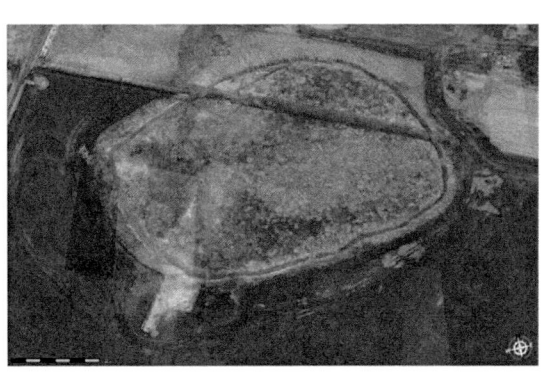 

FIGURE 2. AERIAL VIEW OF THE AMENDOLA DITCH.

FIGURE 3. HOLES AT THE SIDES AND THE BOTTOM OF THE AMENDOLA DITCH.

sourcing and collection (the aquifer is frequent in the 'Amendola sands' porous layers) (Gravina 1980, p. 343-347). Furthermore, in sandy and clay deposits (it is difficult to tell if they were alluvial

FIGURE 4. MASSES OF BLOCKS AND ROCK FRAGMENTS IN THE FILLING OF THE AMENDOLA DITCH
AND COMPARISON TO THE TRENCH OF PASSO DI CORVO SITE.

or intentional fills), a few re-cuts have been recognised, probably a form of maintenance or reuse, without altering the original ditch cut.

In the filling sediments, masses of blocks and rock fragments lay at the same depth along the perimeter. The micromorphological analysis conducted by Andrea Zerboni of the University of Milan demonstrated that the coarse clasts suffered rolling and dragging which preceded the deposit formation. Therefore, the community could have concurrently thrown these heaps of material in the trench, before leaving the site.[3] It is possible that the community of this settlement used pebbles and rock fragments, which were left after the dig of the ditch, in order to build some small stone walls protecting its edges (Figure 4). It is thus possible that the walls contained the terrain pressure and prevented or delayed the infilling of the ditch (Tiné 1983, p. 53). We know a few similar cases in the Tavoliere region: Passo di Corvo I – Campo di Fiori (trenches I-II), and Masseria Candelaro phase II (middle ditch) (Marconi *et al.* 2004, p. 60). At Passo di Corvo III (trench VII), where the excavators found under the surface soil two courses of a stone wall, set in a herringbone pattern, along the inner lip of the feature (Trump 1987 p. 125-127).

Within the ditch, no walls were unearthed: evidently, it was not necessary to close any segments of the structure, with stone walls. It is worth noting that during the excavation works in internal and external areas we found no anthropic soil, floor remains, postholes, pits or other features indicative of settlement activities in the closest surrounding area, there was only this enclosure ditch.

The archaeological artefacts are quite scant compared to the extent of the area. Potsherds are from coarse and fine ware (Figure 5). There are several coarse ware fragments decorated with digital impressions (finger or nail), pinching, rockers or traits impressed and incised by occasional

---

[3] Brown (1991) and other scholars admit the possibility of deliberate refillings in the ditched enclosures.

FIGURE 5. 'GUADONE' *FACIES* POTSHERDS (COARSE AND FINE WARE) FROM THE AMENDOLA SITE.

implements (the edge of a shell, wood, bone, lithic flake), usually covering the whole surface. The decoration patterns are asyntactic and organised in rows or geometrical motifs (zigzag, triangles). In some cases, the upper part of the fragment has a red coloured coating ('Red-slipped lips'). Only one sherd retains a plastic anthropomorphous motif. Vessels forms are both closed and open (bowls and cups), with flat base or pedestal and handles.

The fine ware class is less plentiful. Surfaces are smoothed, burnished and decorated with incisions and impressions of organised motifs, obtained with appropriate stamps. Vessels forms are open, with flat or rounded base. The pottery seems to belong to the 'Guadone' *facies*, i.e. to the advanced Impressed ware of the Italian Early Neolithic period (Muntoni 1996; Tiné 2002, p. 139-143; Cassano *et al.* 2004, p. 105-114). The few *figulina* painted potsherds of the later ceramic style of 'Passo di Corvo' seem to be an intrusion, because they belong to surface layers.

Flake *débitage* is characteristic of the lithic assemblage, with the exception of some blades. Raw material is local and Gargano flint. Tools are mostly scrapers and denticulates. Moreover, there are some fragments of grindstone made of sandstone, calcareous picks and daub.

There are no zooarchaeological remains, possibly because of the acidic nature of the sediments. The ditch fillings only had some *Cerastoderma edule* and *Glycymeris* sp. samples and earth gastropod shells (Deith, 1987; Minniti, 2004). No human remains have been found.

Radiocarbon dating[4] assigns the site to the first centuries of the VI millennium Cal BC, confirming the pottery-based chronology. The Amendola single-ditch is among the most ancient sites with 'Guadone'style pottery in the Tavoliere district (Manfredini, Muntoni 2004, p. 463-464).

After the site was abandoned, sediments could have partially filled the ditch by erosion. In a later moment (in the same period of the 'Guadone' *facies*), a few sectors could have been restored.

The use of the entire ditch is still not clear, but the peculiar pits and shallow holes found at the bottom of the trench, suggest a reclaim intervention or a use as quarry for clay in the lower geological levels (Pleistocenic 'Amendola sands'). This is just a hypothesis: it is worth investigating further.

The scarceness of the anthropic artefacts and ecofacts found in the filling layers seems to indicate that the site was not occupied for dwelling use. Possible post-depositional factors cannot erase all the structures of the settlement. Other surveys conducted in the 2014 have confirmed that in the surrounding zone (towards the North, South and East sides) there were no prehistoric occupation features. Compared to other known sites, the Amendola ditch is the feature most distant from a watercourse, in the middle of the Pleistocenic terraces. It could also lie far from the inhabited area and any significant permanent anthropic activities could not have occurred in the area it encloses. Currently, given no further investigations, we suggest for this feature a use as quarry for clay, as a place for water collection or other unknown ritual functions.

In conclusion, the Amendola Air Base ditch is the first example not only of complete excavation but also of systematic survey of a Neolithic enclosure and its surrounding area. Other 11 sites are located at a distance of 3-9 km from the Amendola ditch, known just by surface collections: they have between 1 and 3 enclosure ditches, even with inner compounds. In two cases (Masseria Fonteviva and Passo di Corvo) a few excavation trenches have confirmed the presence of ceramics in the style of 'Guadone' and have identified a more articulated organization in two or three concentric enclosure ditches, during more phases of occupation (Trump 1987).

The settlement of Masseria Montevergine (Troia)

During 7 months between 2013 and 2014, the archaeological supervision for the TOTO Wind Farm works identified a Neolithic village in the high Tavoliere region near the Troia district (Figure 1B). The evidence was partially visible by aerial photography.

---

[4] Radiocarbon dating made by CEDAD lab – University of Salento (Lecce, Italy).
LTL13339A: cal 5850-5670 BC (2σ. charcoal).
LTL13340A: cal 5850-5650 BC (2σ. charcoal).
LTL13342A: cal 5920-5720 BC (2σ. charcoal).
LTL13341A: cal 5920-5720 BC (2σ. charcoal).

The archaeologists Giordana Dinielli, Vincenza Distasi, Isabella Di Perna, Francesco Notarangelo and Tania Quero conducted the excavations, under the scientific direction of the Superintendence for Archaeological Heritage of Puglia (Dr. Annamaria Tunzi). Unfortunately, the investigation proceeded just by little trenches along the road involved in the infrastructure project.

This village extends along an axis of 722 m NE-SW, on a 250-260 m high hill nearby the Sannoro stream; its northern and southern boundaries have been recognised by aerial photographs. The air photo interpretation and the excavation data have shown a settlement organised by irregularly shaped, parallel, inner and outer enclosure ditches (4 in all), open to the river and other internal features cutting the *crusta* bedrock and a conglomerate layer (Figure 6).

The two external ditches lying in the western zone can correspond to the similar pair in the eastern zone. They have the same pattern, with a narrow outer ditch and a large inner one. Another pair of inner ditches is at a distance of about 90 m from the external pair. Their profile can be altered by cave-ins and wall collapse. In the western zone, they are at a distance of 12.6 m from each other and run in a N-S direction. The ditch A is 2.34 m wide and 1.16 m deep; the ditch B is 4.16 m wide and

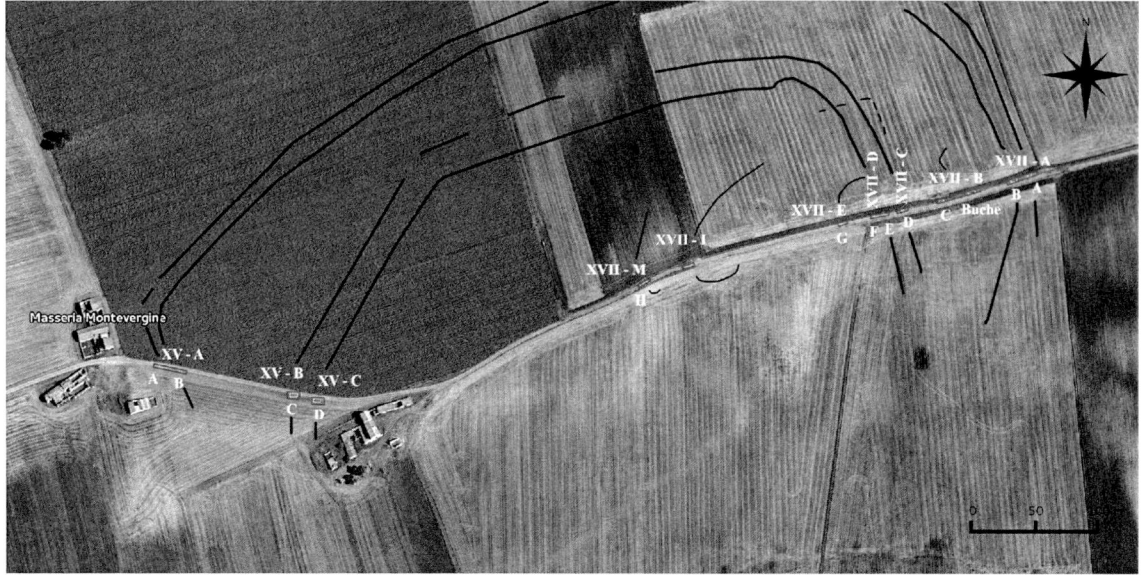

FIGURE 6. AIR PHOTO INTERPRETATION OF THE FEATURES ORGANISATION AT THE MASSERIA MONTEVERGINE SITE.

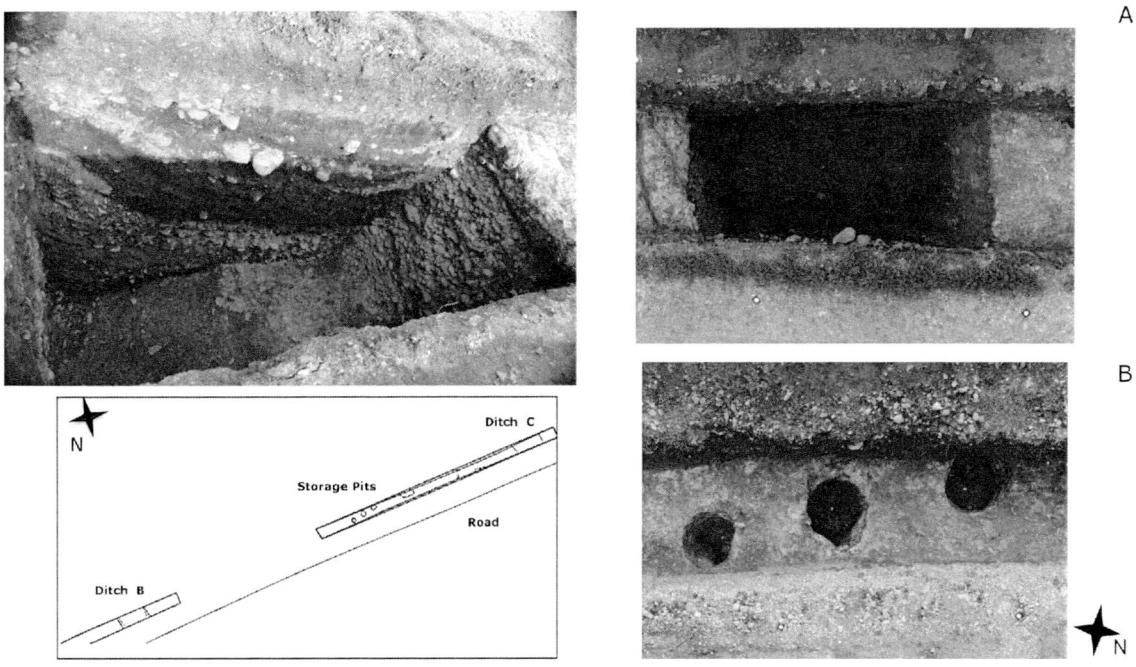

FIGURE 7. VIEW OF SOME FEATURES AT MASSERIA MONTEVERGINE: THE DITCHES E (A), B, C AND THE STORAGE PITS (B), TO THE EAST SIDE.

1.80 m deep from the surface. In the eastern zone, the features are at a distance of 9.4 m and run in a NW-SE direction. The ditch A is 2.74 m wide and 1.80 m deep; the ditch B is 4.06 m wide and 2.50 m deep.

The inner enclosure ditches to the West side are at a distance of about 15 m from each other, in a NE-SW orientation. The ditch C is 3.50 m wide and 2.20 m deep; the ditch D is 3.13 m wide and 2.10 m deep. To the East side the ditches are at a distance of about 12 m from each other, with a NW-SE orientation. The ditch D is 2.54 m wide and about 1 m deep; the ditch E is 4.04 m wide and 2.70 m deep (Figure 7A).

A few piles of blocks and rock fragments have been found in the filling sediments of two ditches (to the West of B, and to the East of E): stones are *crusta* fragments and pebbles/cobbles from the bedrock in which the ditch was dug. Maybe it is a collapse of external small stone walls protecting the edges of the features such as at the Amendola air base, but one cannot exclude that these fragments rolled back into the structure after the inhabitants left the site. The narrow excavation area does not allow to say more. Three round storage pits (0.70 m wide, 0.70-1 m deep, with an axis oriented NE-SW) near a probable small ditch (2.60 m wide, 1.18 m deep) occupy the space included between the two pairs of enclosure ditches (Figure 7B). Other features are two small ditches that could be part of the same C-compound (1.70 m wide, 0.90-1.58 m deep). Two irregular single-ditches lie in the centre of the area, one of which is a concave extremity of a ditch (4.60 m wide, 1.80 m deep); the other one is a large and atypical structure (6 m wide, 0.83 m deep). No burials have been unearthed, but due to the limited surface excavated, it is possible that other features lie within or outside of the area.

During the excavation, neither re-cuts nor reclaims have been documented (apart from Roman period *limites* and square holes), but at this time it is not possible to ascertain if all the features fell into disuse at the same time or if there were other occupation phases and further interventions.

FIGURE 8. 'MASSERIA LA QUERCIA' STYLE POTSHERDS (A) AND
BONE TOOLS (B) FROM MASSERIA MONTEVERGINE SITE.

The excavated trenches produced a rich amount of pottery and lithic artefacts, bones and ecofacts. Coarse ware sherds belong to large vases. Surfaces are often undecorated or with asyntactic or geometrical impressed motifs (digital impressions, pinching, traits and incisions; rocker is rare). In the fine ware class, there is a black-burnished production, and another one with well-organised impressed decorations and 'Masseria La Quercia' style decoration patterns (Tiné 2002, p. 143-148; Cassano *et al.*, 2004, p. 115-143). The latter one consists of painted red or brown geometrical motifs (chevrons, zigzag, grids, checkerboard, trellis, triangles and dots). Red painting, white paste and impressed decorations can occur together on the same surface (Figure 8A). A few sherds seem to present the 'Lagnano da Piede' style, decorated with vertical or oblique painted bands. Furthermore, there is also a certain number of *figulina* painted potsherds of the later ceramic style of 'Passo di Corvo'.

Lithic assemblage presents a flake *débitage*, but there are several blade blanks. Raw material is mainly local flint; the obsidian is present with 7 bladelets (the source is still unknown). The study of the faunal remains is underway: there are domestic ovicaprids, swines/suids and rarely carnivores like dogs. There are bone tools such as needles, awls and one canine tooth pendant (Figure 8B). Some features have returned several fragments of daub. Palaeobotanical analysis on filling sediments are currently underway.

Radiocarbon dates[5] of 13 samples assign the site to the chronological period between the second half of the VI millennium and the first fourth of the V millennium Cal BC. All the inner features date to

---

[5] Radiocarbon dating made by CEDAD lab – University of Salento (Lecce, Italy).
External Western Ditch (A. LTL14190A: cal 5620-5470 BC (2σ. bone).

5630-5320 Cal BC. The enclosure ditches date to 5620-4930 Cal BC. Earlier dating comes from the western area, though the same ditch provides an early date from lower layers and a more recent one from upper levels.

The site lies along a peculiar hill zone of the Subappennino Dauno, far from the plain and the coast. It is at a distance of 5 km from the recently discovered sites of Monte Calvello (Tunzi *et al.* 2008) and Monte San Vincenzo (Tunzi *et al.* 2006). All these settlements reveal a similar inner organisation and they are likely contemporary (even if the Masseria Montevergine context seems to be one of the most recent sites of the 'Masseria La Quercia' *facies*). Besides, Monte San Vincenzo site has a number of the obsidian blades just as Masseria Montevergine settlement: it could be evidence for an exotic raw materials microcircuit in this region.

As a whole, Masseria Montevergine site proves the existence of a settlement system in the hills different from one identified on the coastal plain. For these enclosure ditches is conceivable the 'cliff-castle' system recognised by Bradford by aerial photographs, in other places of the Tavoliere region (as Bovino – La Lamia site, Tunzi 2002, p. 768), i.e. Neolithic settlements, near some slopes, with huge half circles open towards the cliff (Franchin Radcliffe, 2006, p. 91).

Conclusions

These hypogeal structures are very complex and their functions and meanings are still uncertain. The ditch in the Air Base eventually fills a void of knowledge about the Amendola plateau: it forces to consider different uses for this type of construction, other than dwelling activities. The Masseria Candelaro settlement is also significant for its specific organisation confirmed by closely similar sites on the high Tavoliere region. These new data, added to the older studies and the other recent discoveries, may provide further ideas for new research directions on the Neolithic villages of the Tavoliere region.

Aknowledgements

The authors would like to thank Dr. Annick Daneels for accepting this paper and her editing and suggestions. Concerning the Amendola ditch, the Italian Air Force funded new aerial photographs, micromorphological analysis of sediments samples (University of Milan) and radiocarbon dating (CEDAD lab – University of Salento). About the Masseria Montevergine excavations, the air photo interpretation was made by Vincenza Distasi srl; the orthophotos and 3D modelling are in progress by Marco Dilieto srl.

Bibliography

BROWN, K. 1991. A Passion for Excavation. Labour Requirements and Possible Functions for the Ditches of the 'villaggi trincerati' of the Tavoliere, Apulia. The Accordia Research Papers 2: p. 6-30.

BROWN, K. 1995. Social control or 'opium of the people'? The role of religion in the Neolithic of the Tavoliere. In Waldren, W. H.; Ensenyat, J. A.; Kennard, R. C., eds., Ritual, Rites and Religion in Prehistory. IIIrd Deya International Conference of Prehistory. Oxford: B.A.R, p. 184-194. (BAR International Series; 611 I).

CALDARA, M.; PENNETTA, L.; SIMONE, O. 2004. L'ambiente fisico nell'area dell'insediamento. In Cassano, S. M.; Manfredini, A., eds., Masseria Candelaro. Vita quotidiana e mondo ideologico in una comunità neolitica del Tavoliere. Foggia: Grenzi editore. p. 29-42.

External Eastern Ditch (A. LTL14033A: cal 5220-4930 BC (2σ. bone).
Inner Eastern ditch (D. LTL14027A: cal 5370-5200 BC (2σ. charcoal).
Storage pit – LTL14031A: cal 5480-5320 BC (2σ. bone).
C-Compound? (G. LTL14191A: cal 5540-5340 BC (2σ. bone).
Central feature (H. LTL14034A: cal 5630-5480 BC (2σ. bone).

CASSANO, S. M.; MANFREDINI, A., eds. 1983. Studi sul Neolitico del Tavoliere della Puglia. Oxford: B.A.R. (BAR International Series; 160).

CASSANO, S. M.; MANFREDINI, A., eds. 2004. Masseria Candelaro. Vita quotidiana e mondo ideologico in una comunità neolitica del Tavoliere. Foggia: Grenzi editore.

CASSANO, S. M.; ERAMO, G.; LAVIANO, R.; MARCONI, N.; MUNTONI, I. M.; NATALI, E. 2004. La produzione ceramica. In Cassano, S. M.; Manfredini, A., eds., Masseria Candelaro. Vita quotidiana e mondo ideologico in una comunità neolitica del Tavoliere, Claudio Foggia: Grenzi Editore. p. 93-252.

CIARANFI, N. 1983. Osservazioni geologiche e morfologiche sull'entroterra del Golfo di Manfredonia. In Cassano, S.M.; Manfredini, A., eds., Studi sul Neolitico del Tavoliere della Puglia. Oxford: B.A.R., p. 203-219 (BAR International Series; 160).

DEITH, M. R. 1987. La raccolta dei molluschi nel Tavoliere in epoca preistorica. In Cassano, S. M.; Cazzella, A.; Manfredini, A.; Moscoloni, M., eds., Coppa Nevigata e il suo territorio. Testimonianze archeologiche dal VII al II millennio a. C. Roma: Quasar. p. 101-106.

DELANO SMITH, C. 1983. Il clima durante il Neolitico. In Tiné, S., ed., Passo di Corvo e la civiltà neolitica del Tavoliere. Genova: Sagep Editrice. p. 11-21.

FRANCHIN RADCLIFFE, F. 2006. Paesaggi sepolti in Daunia. John Bradford e la ricerca archeologica dal cielo. Foggia: Claudio Grenzi Editore.

GRAVINA, A. 1980. Annotazioni sui fossati e sulle strutture ipogeiche dei villaggi neolitici della Daunia settentrionale. Rivista di Scienze Preistoriche 35, p. 339-355.

JONES, G. D. B. 1987. Apulia. Neolithic Settlement in the Tavoliere, Vol. 1. London: Society of Antiquaries of London.

MANFREDINI, A.; MUNTONI, I. 2004. La cronologia. In Cassano, S. M.; Manfredini, A. eds. – Masseria Candelaro. Vita quotidiana e mondo ideologico in una comunità neolitica del Tavoliere. Foggia: Claudio Grenzi Editore. p. 463-468.

MARCONI, N.; MUNTONI, I. M.; CASSANO, S. M.; MANFREDINI, A.; CARBONI, G.; CURCI, A. 2004. Le strutture e le stratigrafie. In Cassano, S. M.; Manfredini, A., eds., Masseria Candelaro. Vita quotidiana e mondo ideologico in una comunità neolitica del Tavoliere. Foggia: Claudio Grenzi Editore. p. 49-91.

MINNITI, C. 2004. I resti di molluschi marini. In Cassano, S. M.; Manfredini, A., eds., Masseria Candelaro. Vita quotidiana e mondo ideologico in una comunità neolitica del Tavoliere. Foggia: Claudio Grenzi Editore. p. 441-444.

MONACO, A. 2011. A simulation of farming and breeding activities: comparing the economic strategies in South East Italy Neolithic communities. Origini 33, p. 61-81.

MUNTONI, I. M. 1996. Ceramica. Coppa Nevigata e Masseria Candelaro. In Tiné, V., ed., Forme e tempi della neolitizzazione in Italia Meridionale e in Sicilia. Soveria Mannelli: Rubbettino editore. Vol. 1, p. 269-276.

RADINA, F.; SARTI, L. 2002. Le strutture d'abitato. In Fugazzola Delpino, M. A.; Pessina, A.; Tiné, V., eds., Le ceramiche impresse nel Neolitico antico. Italia e Mediterraneo. Studi di Paletnologia. Roma: Istituto poligrafico e Zecca dello Stato. Vol. 1, p. 196-207.

SKEATS, R. 2000. The Social Dynamics of Enclosure in the Neolithic of the Tavoliere, South-East Italy, Journal of Mediterranean Archaeology 13: 2, p. 155-188.

TINÉ, S. 1983. Passo di Corvo e la civiltà neolitica del Tavoliere. Genova: Sagep Editrice.

TINÉ, V. 2002. Le facies a ceramica impressa dell'Italia meridionale e della Sicilia. In Fugazzola Delpino, M. A.; Pessina, A.; Tiné, V. eds. – Le ceramiche impresse nel Neolitico antico. Italia e Mediterraneo. Studi di Paletnologia. Roma: Istituto poligrafico e Zecca dello Stato. Vol., p. 132-165.

TRUMP, D. H. 1987. The excavated sites. Excavations in 1949-1963. In Jones, G. D. B., ed., Apulia. Neolithic Settlement in the Tavoliere. London: Society of Antiquaries of London. Vol. 1, p. 117-135.

TUNZI, A. M. 2002. Il territorio dauno. In Fugazzola Delpino, M. A.; Pessina, A.; Tiné, V., eds., Le ceramiche impresse nel Neolitico antico. Italia e Mediterraneo. Studi di Paletnologia. Roma: Istituto poligrafico e Zecca dello Stato. Vol. 1, p. 767-774.

TUNZI SISTO, A. M; DANESI, M.; SIMONETTI, R. 2006. Il grande abitato neolitico di Troia – Monte S. Vincenzo. In Gravina, A., ed., 26° Convegno Nazionale sulla Preistoria – Protostoria – Storia della Daunia. San Severo, 10-11 dicembre 2005. Atti. San Severo: Archeoclub d'Italia. p. 39-57.

TUNZI SISTO, A. M.; MONACO, A.; SIMONETTI, R. 2008. Lo scavo sistematico di un fossato a C: il caso del villaggio neolitico di Monte Calvello. In Gravina, A., ed., 28° Convegno Nazionale sulla Preistoria – Protostoria – Storia della Daunia. San Severo 25-26 novembre 2007. Atti. San Severo: Archeoclub d'Italia. p. 29-48.

TUNZI SISTO, A. M.; QUERO, T. (in press). Il Neolitico antico nell'Aeroporto Militare 'Luigi Rovelli' – Amendola (FG): lo scavo integrale di un fossato perimetrale. In Gravina, A., ed., 34° Convegno Nazionale sulla Preistoria – Protostoria – Storia della Daunia, San Severo 16-17 novembre 2013. San Severo: Archeoclub d'Italia.

First test for luminescence dating of ancient mud-brick buildings from Northern Mesopotamia

Jorge SANJURJO-SÁNCHEZ
University Institute of Geology 'Isidro Parga Pondal', University of A Coruña,
Campus de Elviña, 15071 A Coruña, Spain
jsanjurjo@udc.es

Juan-Luis MONTERO FENOLLÓS
Department of Humanities, University of A Coruña, Campus de Esteiro,
15403 Ferrol, Spain
fenollos@udc.es

Abstract

Raw earth has been used since Prehistory to make sun-dried mud-bricks that cannot usually be dated, as they do not preserve organic matter. However, they contain abundant silicate minerals typically used for luminescence dating, although this technique still has not been tested on mud-bricks or earthen buildings. In stone-poor Mesopotamia, most buildings were constructed with mud-bricks. We have performed the first luminescence tests on earthen structures from two archaeological sites of the Middle Euphrates Valley and compared results with other dates obtained for charcoal, pottery and sediments. Results show that mud-bricks are reliable targets for luminescence dating.

Keywords: *adobe, Middle Euphrates, luminescence, Syria, chronology*

Résumé

Premiers essais de datation par thermoluminescence de briques d'argile crues de la Mésopotamie Septentrionale

La terre a été utilisée en Mésopotamie depuis la Préhistoire pour fabriquer des briques séchées au soleil, qui ne peuvent être généralement datées, étant donné qu'elles ne conservent pas des restes de matière organique (de la paille notamment). Cependant, la brique est riche en divers minéraux de silice, qui peuvent être utilisés pour la datation par luminescence; mais cette technique n'a pas encore été testée sur les murs en briques crues de l'architecture du Proche-Orient ancien. En Mésopotamie, la plupart des bâtiments ont été construits en brique, en raison de l'absence de pierre dans la région. Nous avons effectué les premiers tests de luminescence sur des briques de deux sites archéologiques de la vallée du Moyen Euphrate syrien. Les dates obtenues ont été comparées avec d'autres datations (charbon de bois, céramique et sédiments) et les résultats montrent que la brique est un élément fiable pour la datation par luminescence.

Mots-clés: *adobe, Moyen Euphrate, luminescence, Syrie, chronologie*

Introduction

Building chronologies in archaeology is a complex problem that is commonly underestimated. It is quite common practice to assign an age to an archaeological site by dating one of a few samples by a single absolute dating method. In some cases the application of the absolute dating method is poorly understood and even leads to misleading conclusions. This is still more problematic in the case of sites that were occupied by humans in several phases of variable time span. The assignation of an age or a chronology to an archaeological site depends on several questions including age, age range, occupation phases, the type of material dated and methods used to get absolute ages. For example, if an ancient urban centre were occupied by a civilization during a time span of about 600 years it is not the same if the age of the site is 3600-3000 years BC than 400 BC-200 CE (expressed in calendar years). The precision and accuracy of several dating methods (e.g. radiocarbon, luminescence, archaeomagnetism) will determine the results of the chronological analysis. Moreover, the meaning of the age of an object depends on its nature. It is not the same dating charcoal, wood or pottery (all of which theoretically provide the age of occupation) than a sediment (theoretically dating occupation or post-occupation) or a building material (theoretically indicative of initial occupation).

Age results can differ depending on the dating methods used. An example of this is the use of radiocarbon in Mesopotamia. Radiocarbon is usually applied on charcoal samples to get absolute ages. However, some trees can contain wood of age ranges from 100 to 1000 years. In ancient Mesopotamian civilizations wood was a valuable material that was commonly reused for building. Thus, it is possible that the use of wood or charcoal (from burned wood) provides ages much older than the age of the archaeological event that one wants to date (Sanjurjo-Sánchez, 2012, 2015). Thus, it is very relevant to apply absolute dating methods to other building materials. In the case of a large occupation span for a site, the age of a building will give us an age that we can compare with other objects to get accurate time ranges for the occupation of the site.

Dating building materials

Traditional building materials provide valuable information on the past of ancient and historical buildings. Studies on the characterisation of such materials provides information on the origin of raw materials, manufacture and building technologies, or decay of materials. However, one of the most important potential values is the possibility to apply absolute dating techniques to such materials. Applying dating methods will provide information on different building phases and periods (chronology).

Among traditional non-organic building materials, bricks and mortars are particularly interesting and several methods have developed specific procedures to apply them. Luminescence dating has probably been the most frequently used method for dating fired bricks. It has also been applied to dating mortars with important success in the last four years (Sanjurjo-Sánchez, 2012, 2015). Radiocarbon has also been applied to lime mortars with relative success. However, they have not been applied to mud-bricks, despite the fact that luminescence is currently applied to similar inorganic materials (Aitken, 1985) and it is a potential tool to acquire chronologies from this type of material. Mud-brick was used in ancient and historic times (up to present times in most parts of the World). In the case of Mesopotamian architecture, mud-brick is the most abundant material and thus its potential use for chronologies is very high if dating is reliable. In Mesopotamia other materials such as wood are problematic due to the problems mentioned above, while fired bricks are scarce and the reliability of other materials such as gypsum mortars is still low as special procedures to date them have not been developed.

Mud-brick in Mesopotamia

Mesopotamia is considered as a land of mud and mud-brick architecture from the earliest phases of settlements (Neolithic). The scarcity of other building materials and the abundance of mud-rich soils (raw earth from alluvial plains) is probably the most important cause of this. Moreover, the summer conditions with high temperatures and low humidity is appropriate for making sun-dried bricks. Even when fired bricks (or baked bricks) are known, mud-bricks were still used (probably because of the cost of fuel to burn them).

In the oldest Neolithic settlements the first mud-bricks were hand-shaped as cigars and loaves of variable sizes. However, from the 5th millennium mud-bricks were rectangular with regular and constant shapes, made in wooden moulds open at the top and bottom. The most frequently used raw materials were clay-rich soil, chopped straw or dung temper. Such materials were puddled with water for consistency, moulded and sundried (Moorey, 1999; Sauvage 1998). Though its imprint remains, the organic matter itself was not preserved most of the times. Thus, radiocarbon dating is not applicable for these materials after a lapse of time of some centuries or thousands of years. However, luminescence dating should be applicable if quartz or feldspar is present.

Considering such information and both the large time span of continuous or discontinuous occupation of some archaeological sites of Mesopotamia and the problems related above on the use of some dating methods and materials, dating mud-bricks should be a crucial task in order to get more precise chronologies for this area starting from the Neolithic. Table 1 summarises the problems arising from the use of some materials for dating and dating methods.

Building material	Raw material	Use	Chronology	Dating method	Routinely dated?
Mud-bricks	Mud and chaff	Foundation, Wall, Roof	9th Millennium	Luminescence?	No
Mortars	Gypsum	Plasters, Renders, joint Mortars	9th Millennium	Luminescence?	No
Mortars	Calcite	Plasters, Renders, joint Mortars, Whitewash	9th Millennium	Radiocarbon, Luminescence	Yes
Blocks	Stone	Foundation, Walls	>10,000 BC?	Luminescence?	No
Ceramic (bricks, tiles)	Clay & temper	Foundation, Walls, Roof	7th Millennium	Luminescence	Yes
Reeds	Reed/plants	Roof, Walls	>7th Millennium?	Radiocarbon	Yes
Wood	Wood	Timbers for Walls, Roofs, Pillars	>10,000 BC?	Dendrochronology, Radiocarbon	Yes

TABLE 1. BUILDING MATERIALS, MAIN RAW MATERIALS, FUNCTION AND CHRONOLOGY OF USE BY CIVILIZATIONS WITH MENTION OF THE DATING METHOD THAT CAN BE APPLIED TO DATE THEM.

Luminescence dating of building materials

Luminescence is the emission of light from crystalline materials (minerals). Naturally occurring radioactivity causes the excitation of atoms within a mineral crystal lattice. As a consequence electrons are activated at higher energy states and some of them are captured at levels called 'electron traps'. With increased time, more and more electrons will be captured at the traps and so the luminescence signal will increase at a constant rate (Aitken, 1985). Since the number of traps is limited, the luminescence will reach a saturation value (saturation dose). The release of trapped electrons occurs in the form of light (luminescence) and requires a stimulus.

The intensity of light emitted by a mineral is proportional to the amount of electrons trapped, and therefore to the energy received by the mineral due to radioactive exposure since the signal was zeroed for the last time. Such correlation allows us to calculate the time period elapsed from the last zeroing (Aitken, 1985). The trapped electrons stored within minerals can be released in the laboratory producing a luminescence signal. Heating mineral samples releases the trapped electrons and the resulting signal emission is called thermoluminescence (TL). When a mineral is stimulated by light, traps are emptied in a few seconds, and the measured signal is called optically stimulated luminescence (OSL).

Although different minerals can be used for luminescence dating, this method is usually limited to quartz and feldspars due to their ubiquity in archaeological objects. Quartz is considered to be the most adequate mineral for luminescence dating. Its luminescence properties are relatively well known and the signal is not affected by the phenomenon termed anomalous fading that occurs with some feldspars. There are a few circumstances when quartz may not be a suitable mineral for dating:

when absent, when it contains feldspar inclusions that complicate the luminescence signal, when it shows a low signal or sensitivity changes, or anomalous fading (in the case of volcanic quartz) (Bonde et al. 2001), or when the dose reaches saturation (after some tens of thousands of years of burial).

The luminescence age equation is the ratio between the measured total absorbed dose (estimated as equivalent dose by luminescence) and the dose-rate of ionizing radiation in the sample and the environment surrounding the dated material. The calculated age of the dated material is the time elapsed since the last exposure to sunlight or heat before burial (Aitken, 1985). Thus:

$$\text{Age} = \text{ED (Gy)} / \text{DR (Gy/ka)}$$

Where ED is the Equivalent Dose and DR the dose rate. The equivalent dose is an estimation of the total energy accumulated by the measured minerals from the last exposure to light or heat. It is usually measured in Gray (Gy).

The dose rate is the energy delivered by each unit of time (year of ka) from ionizing radiation within the sample and the surrounding environment. Naturally ionising radiation occurs in the form of alpha and beta particles, gamma radiation and cosmic rays. Such ionizing radiation occurs due to the natural radioactivity of the dated materials and the surrounding environment. The radioactivity can be assessed in terms of dose rate of radioactivity received per unit of time (Aitken, 1985). Such radioactivity is due to the content of uranium (U), thorium (Th) and potassium (^{40}K) in the samples and surrounding environment. Cosmic rays are produced by ionising cosmic radiation and can be estimated from geographic position, altitude and burial depth of the sampled material (Prescott and Hutton, 1994). The effect of the different types of radiation on the dose rates is not the same. Thus, alpha particles typically travel a few microns through geological and archaeological materials (such as ceramics), while beta particles reach a few millimetres. Gamma rays reach about 30 cm. Thus, gamma and cosmic rays constitute the external dose while beta and alpha (and partially gamma) the internal dose.

There are three methods to determine the dose rate: direct *in situ* measurement using dosimeters or gamma spectrometry that measure the dose rate using counting devices, or by determination using conversion factors after chemical analysis of U, Th and U concentrations in the materials. In any case, some assumptions are made to get reliable final ages (Aitken, 1985): the radionuclide concentrations are constant in time, the material is homogeneous and the system is an infinite matrix.

Although luminescence dating is currently applied on fired bricks, and lime mortars have been dated in recent years (Sanjurjo-Sánchez, 2012, 2015), the most frequently dated materials are sediments. The luminescence age of sediments provides the time elapsed since the deposition and burial of the dated sediment. The daylight exposure of the sediment minerals before burial is the cause of the zeroing of the geological luminescence signal. In the case of mud-bricks, the use of clay and soils to produce the mud-bricks (and the extraction, transport, wash, mixture, etc. of the mud) causes the exposure of minerals to daylight. Thus, luminescence dating could be used although it still has not been tested.

Archaeological Background

The study of mud-bricks has been performed in two archaeological sites of the Middle Syrian Euphrates Valley in the Deir ez-Zor district. In this area the reported archaeological data have been scarce but the study of both sites has provided valuable chronological information using radiocarbon ages from charcoal samples and luminescence ages from sediments and pottery.

Tall Abu Fahd (TAF) is located at the end of the Khanuqa gorge on the left side of the Euphrates River (Figure 1), next to the Abu Fahd Village (Syria). There is a wall of basaltic ashlars on the surface and

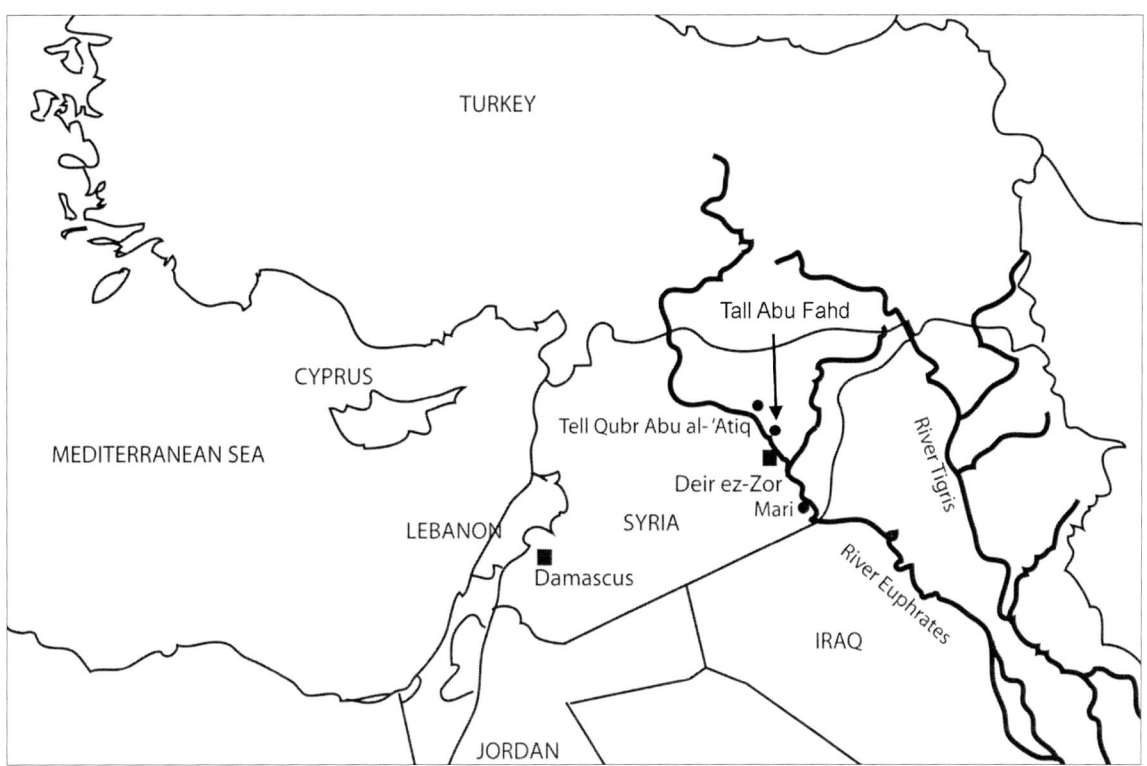

FIGURE 1. MAP OF NEAR EAST AND LOCATION OF THE SITES IN THE MIDDLE EUPHRATES.

a rectangular tower in the North Eastern corner. Though the pottery fragments correspond to Middle Bronze Age II (1800-1650 BC), luminescence dating of sediments and pottery, and radiocarbon dating of charcoal (ages calibrated with Oxcal) indicated an occupation of the site at least since 1610-1410 BC and destruction at least around 680±240 BC, calendar years (Sanjurjo-Sánchez et al., 2008). In this site, there still remains a tower of basalt blocks and adjacent mud-brick walls (Figure 2). Two mud-bricks of such walls have been sampled for luminescence dating.

Tell Qubr Abu al-'Atiq (TQ) is an archaeological site located on the hilltop of a Quaternary cliff on the left bank of the Euphrates, overlooking the river and controlling the access to the Khanuqa Gorge. As an abandoned old river branch remains at the foot of the cliff, this settlement was a potential key site for territory control in the Middle Euphrates valley (Montero Fenollós 2010 and 2014). There are two different areas in the site. The western corner of the tell rises above the level of a 'lower city' that apparently only experienced one phase of occupation during the Early Bronze Age, based on typological pottery classification. Excavations have shown extensive occupation of this part during the Early Dynastic II-III period (2700-2350 BC, calendar years).

The excavation brought to light the north, west and south walls of an almost square room, with a doorway in the south wall. The floor and the inside walls of the room were plastered with gypsum (Figure 2). Outside the northern wall of the rooms was an uncovered level of grey mud, small pebbles and ash, possibly part of the surface revetment of a street that ran along the building to the north. A minor excavation in the NW corner revealed that the foundation of the street consisted of two layers of medium-sized uneven stones, namely of basalt, gypsum and limestone, directly placed on the original surface without foundation ditch.

The reconstruction of the chronology based on luminescence of pottery, sediments and calibrated radiocarbon ages of charcoals (Sanjurjo-Sánchez and Montero Fenollós, 2012) indicate that human

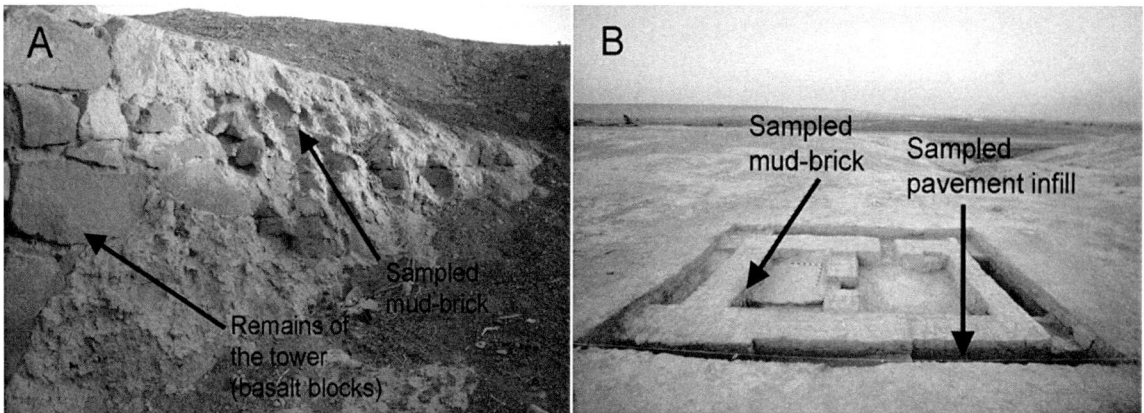

FIGURE 2. PICTURES OF THE SAMPLED CONSTRUCTIONS: (A) REMAINING WALL IN TALL ABU FAHD AND SAMPLED MUD-BRICK; (B) POSITION OF SAMPLES FROM TELL QUBR ABU AL-'ATIQ.

occupation fits the archaeological hypothesis providing an older and maximum occupation period between 2840 and 2340 BC (Early Bronze Age) and a younger period between 1400 and 900 BC (that overlaps the Late Bronze Age).

Aim of the study

In this work we reveal the first results of applying luminescence dating to mud-bricks from two buildings of different sites and periods of the Middle Euphrates Valley. Luminescence still has not been tested on mud-bricks or earthen buildings. We compare the results with other chronological data obtained from radiocarbon and luminescence dating of other materials of the same sites. We also date the infill of a pavement on the floor of one of the sites to test results.

Methods

To collect mud-brick samples for luminescence dating, PVC cores 50 cm long and 5 cm in diameter were hammered into the mud-bricks from the surface of walls (Figure 2).

The sediment cores were opened under special conditions required for luminescence dating (in subdued red Light) in the Luminescence Lab of the University of A Coruña (Spain). Grains from the central part of the cores were used for luminescence analyses. Sand grains were obtained by sieving and coarse quartz extracted by the methods detailed in Sanjurjo-Sánchez and Montero Fenollós (2012).

A blue-OSL (BL-OSL) single-aliquot regenerative dose (SAR) protocol was used to estimate the equivalent dose of quartz grains (Murray and Wintle, 2000, 2003). All measurements were made on an automated Risø TL/OSL-DA-15 reader equipped with an EMI 9635 QA photomultiplier tube and using an internal $^{90}Sr/^{90}Y$ source that provides 0.120±0.003 Gy/s. Grains were mounted on stainless steel discs using silicone spray and the light emission was measured using an optical filter Hoya U-340.

The annual dose rates (Aitken, 1985) were estimated in the laboratory using High-Resolution γ-Spectrometry (HRGS) for the sediment samples. Conversion factors of Guerin *et al.* (2011) were used to estimate annual dose rates from quartz grains neglecting the alpha dose. Cosmic dose rates were estimated from Prescott and Hutton (1994).

Results and Discussion

The resulting ages from the area studied in Tell Qubr Abu al-'Atiq reveals that the absolute chronology fits the ages inferred by studying the stylistic features of pottery, but they provide more detailed information about the occupation, time span and destruction or abandonment of the site (table 2). While typological studies of pottery placed the occupation of the site between 4700 and 4350 BP, radiocarbon ages of charcoal indicated occupation between 4850 and 4350 BP. The OSL dating of the sediments provide two ages: 4160±280 BP and 3790±210 BP. Such ages fit between 4000 and 3880 BP. As the sediment is formed by the destruction of mud-brick walls, leading to the bleaching of the coarse quartz (present within the mud-bricks matrix) by daylight, this age indicates the abandonment or destruction of the site in such period. Thus, we cannot discard that the occupation of the site was extended up to such period as it is not possible to know if the charcoal ages correspond to the period of occupation or to older ages due to reuse of wood. In this site, one mud-brick and a pavement were dated by OSL. The age of the mud-brick indicates an age range of 4380-4140 BP, consistent with occupation; this would indicate that the original wood of the charcoal samples could have been reused. However, the pavement age range is 4700-4120 BP, indicating that the dating of this structure's building material can provide reliable ages that fit the occupation of the site.

Sample	Site	Material	Method	Age (ka)
TQA.08.B-1	Tell Qubr Abu al-'Atiq	Charcoal	Radiocarbon	4470±120
TQA.08.B-2	Tell Qubr Abu al-'Atiq	Charcoal	Radiocarbon	4660±190
TQA.08.B3-sed	Tell Qubr Abu al-'Atiq	Sediment	OSL	4200±280
TQA.08.B4-sed	Tell Qubr Abu al-'Atiq	Sediment	OSL	3830±210
TQB.09.A1	Tell Qubr Abu al-'Atiq	Mud-brick	OSL	4250±120
TQB.09.T0	Tell Qubr Abu al-'Atiq	Pavement	OSL	4410±290
TAF-1	Tell Abu Fahd	Sediment	OSL	2640±240
TAF-2	Tell Abu Fahd	Sediment	OSL	2680±240
TAF.06.P.N4.2	Tell Abu Fahd	Pottery	TL	2640±640
TAF-C	Tell Abu Fahd	Charcoal	Radiocarbon	3220±40
TAF.09.A1	Tell Abu Fahd	Mud-brick	OSL	3110±200
TAF.09.A2	Tell Abu Fahd	Mud-brick	OSL	3650±450

TABLE 2. AGES OBTAINED FROM THE OBJECTS DATED IN THE TWO SITES STUDIED.

The ages obtained from Tell Abu Fahd samples provide a more precise chronology than that obtained from typological features of pottery (table 2). Ceramic typology reveals the possible occupation between 3800 and 2650 BP. A radiocarbon age of a charcoal sample indicates occupation between 3610 and 3410 BP that fits a TL age obtained from a pottery fragment that ranges between 3280 and 2000 BP, a too large time span but that limits the occupation to an age range of 3280-2650 BP (calibrated age) if the charcoal did not correspond to reused wood. The OSL ages obtained from sediments date the destruction/abandonment of the site between 2880 and 2440 BP. If radiocarbon provides an occupation age, that is if the sample did not correspond to reused wood, then that means that the site was inhabited during more than 400 years. This is consistent with the mud-brick ages that provide an age range between 3310 and 2910 BP for occupation.

In conclusion, mud-bricks and earthen constructions (including the infill of pavements) seem to be reliable materials for absolute dating by Luminescence (OSL). It seems to provide a more reliable dating for such structures than charcoal, pottery or sediments caused by the destruction of buildings, if one intends to get the age of founding and occupation of a site. Moreover, no alternative methods exist to directly date such building structures (walls) and foundations if organic matter is not present.

Acknowledgements

This research was funded by projects 'Investigaciones Arqueológicas en el Medio Éufrates' (HAR210-15866, Ministry of Economy and Competitiveness, Spain) and 'Expedición arqueolóxica da UDC no Medio Éufrates Sirio' (10PXIB 167197PR, Xunta de Galicia, Spain).

Bibliography

AITKEN, M. J. 1985. Thermoluminescence Dating. London: Academic Press. 359 p.

BONDE, A. [et al.] 2001. Santorini: Luminescence dating of a volcanic province using quartz? Quaternary Science Reviews, 20, p. 789-793.

GUERIN, G. [et al.] 2011. Dose-rate conversion factors: update, Ancient TL, 29, p. 5-8.

MOOREY, P. R. S. 1999. Ancient Mesopotamian Materials and Industries the Archaeological Evidence. Winona Lake (Indiana): Einsenbrauns. 414 p.

MONTERO FENOLLÓS, J. L. [et al.] 2010. Tell Qubr Abu al-'Atiq: from an early Dynastic city to a Middle Assyrian Fort. Aula Orientalis, 28, p. 73-84.

MONTERO FENOLLÓS, J. L. 2014. 'Mari et le verrou de Khanuqa: frontière politique et territoire aux IIIe et IIe millénaires av. J.-C.'. Syria Supplément 2, p. 231-246.

MURRAY, A. S.; WINTLE, A. G. 2000. Luminescence dating of quartz using an improved single-aliquot regenerative-dose protocol. Radiation Measurements, 32, p. 57-73.

MURRAY, A. S.; WINTLE, A. G. 2003. The single aliquot regenerative dose protocol: potential for improvements in reliability. Radiation Measurements, 37:4-5, p. 377-381.

PRESCOTT, J. R.; HUTTON, J. T. 1994. Cosmic ray contributions to dose rates for luminescence and ESR dating: large depths and long-term time variations. Radiation Measurements, 23, 2/3, p. 497-500.

SANJURJO-SÁNCHEZ, J. [et al.] 2008. TL/OSL dating of sediment and pottery from two Syrian archaeological sites. Geochronometria, 31, p. 21-27.

SANJURJO-SÁNCHEZ, J. 2012. Dating bricks and mortars of ancient and historical buildings. In S. M. Rivera; A. L. Pena Diaz eds., Brick and mortar research. New York: Nova Science Publishers, p. 171-194.

SANJURJO-SÁNCHEZ, J. 2015. Dating historical buildings: an update on the possibilities of absolute dating methods. International Journal of Architectural Heritage, DOI: 10.1080/15583058.2015.1055384.

SANJURJO-SÁNCHEZ, J.; MONTERO FENOLLÓS, J. L. 2012. Chronology during the Bronze Age in the archaeological site Tell Qubr Abu al-'Atiq, Syria. Journal of Archaeological Science, 39, p. 163-174.

SAUVAGE, M. 1998. La brique et sa mise en œuvre en Mésopotamie, Paris: ERC. 227 p.

Traditional Architecture and Socio-Political Organization at Figuig Oasis, Morocco

Florencia Tatiana Azul Ultramar RAMÍREZ-RODRÍGUEZ
Mohamed I University, Faculty of Science, Oujda City, Morocco
azulramirez108@gmail.com

Abstract

Figuig Oasis, located in Eastern Morocco, is a settlement whose ancient core is mainly composed of earthen household units and walled gardens. Historical accounts suggest that it was founded in early Islamic times by Amazigh (also called Berbers) tribes. This paper is primarily concerned with the relation between ancient socio-political organization and architectural layout and technology. The first type of analysis concerns the general settlement pattern, while the second refers to traditional building materials and collective work.

Keywords: *Traditional earthen architecture, tangible and intangible cultural heritage, segmentary socio-political organization, settlement pattern.*

Résumé

Architecture traditionnelle et organisation sociopolitique à l'Oasis de Figuig, Maroc

L'Oasis de Figuig, situé à l'est du Maroc, est un établissement humain dont les quartiers les plus anciens sont composés de logements et des jardins clôturés bâtis en terre crue. Les données historiques suggèrent qu'il a été fondé au début de l'époque islamique par certaines tribus Amazigh (dites aussi berbères). Cet article analyse la relation entre l'ancienne organisation sociopolitique et le tracé urbain ainsi que la technologie de construction. Le premier type d'analyse concerne le plan général de l'établissement, tandis que le deuxième vise les matériaux et les procédés de construction traditionnels.

Mots-clés: *Architecture de terre, patrimoine culturel tangible et intangible, organisation sociopolitique segmentaire, organisation du territoire.*

Introduction

The Figuig Oasis is located in Eastern Morocco, at a distance of about 400 km. from the Mediterranean coast of the meridian that crosses the city of Oujda, two kilometers closer from the Algerian border. The settlement is about 600 to 700 hectare and has some 15,000 inhabitants (Figure 1). The region has a 'Saharan Climate', with a temperature variation between an average low in January of 3.8°C, and an average high of 41.3°C in July. Under these conditions, earthen architecture is the best strategy to create an artificial environment favorable to human survival due to the thermal attributes of earth, which retains heat in the winter and is cool in the summer.

Though earth is used as a building material throughout the world, human inventiveness is not the same everywhere; this means that traditional architecture is not only circumscribed by regional weather and geology, but to cultural and historical particularities. Therefore, different approaches can be adopted to study traditional architecture, as for example, from technical or aesthetic points of view. Nevertheless, in this paper our interest will be the historical and cultural particularities that shaped the traditional fortified architecture that characterized Figuig oasis during a long time, particularly with respect to the design and function of the urban complex, in the socio-political organization context, as well as the labor needed to build and maintain these earthen structures. Therefore, our research strategy included the compilation of oral traditions to understand several aspects of this settlement.

Thus, the term 'Traditional Architecture' will be understood here, following UNESCO parameters, as a cultural heritage that has a tangible and an intangible dimension. It refers to building methods

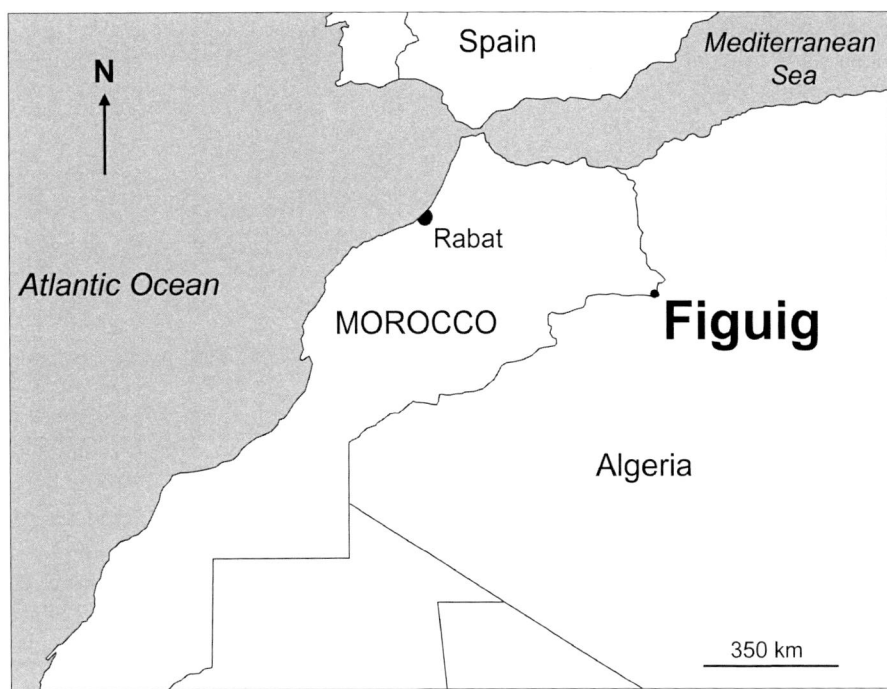

FIGURE 1. LOCATION OF FIGUIG OASIS IN MOROCCO (DRAWING FROM GOOGLE EARTH CONTOUR).

developed through time, from a corpus of unwritten knowledge that is transmitted from one generation to another, in practical and oral way.

From this point of view, the principal features of traditional architectural are the following: 1) its building materials consist mainly of local resources; in Figuig those materials are: earth, sub products of palm, wood of various local trees, lime and plants mixed with other natural elements (that are used to produce paints and insect repellents that act to preserve wooden artefacts); 2) the procedures to 'choose and prepare' the building materials mentioned above are part of a cultural heritage where technical knowledge is tied to a local worldview that gives rise to particular cultural practices, and 3) the general design of these constructions (houses, religious and/or administrative buildings, defensive walls, garden enclosures, etc.) conform to the sociopolitical organization that prevailed at the time they were built. In the same way, designs, orientation and internal space distribution constitute elements that reflect religious beliefs and group identity.

Summing up, traditional architecture may be defined as a 'historical and archaeological heritage', since in these fields, innovations and modifications in dwellings and other buildings, usually reflect social, political, historical, economical, and religious transformations of any given society.

Historical accounts

The Figuig oasis, as all other oases located on the northern fringe of the Sahara, may be described as a culturally modified ecosystem (Pastor *et al.* 2012:103), achieved by adapting palm trees to a desert environment where climate and ecological characteristics represent a challenge to human survival (Figure 2). Actually no less than 16 species of date palms and other fruit trees and vegetables are grown at the oasis.

Figuig is part of the oasis belt aligned parallel to the North African Mediterranean coast, in contact with the Sahara desert biome, located between the arid and hyper arid bioclimate (Seva *et al.* 2012:43), therefore, nomad populations and travelers, still refers to it as a door to the Sahara. The

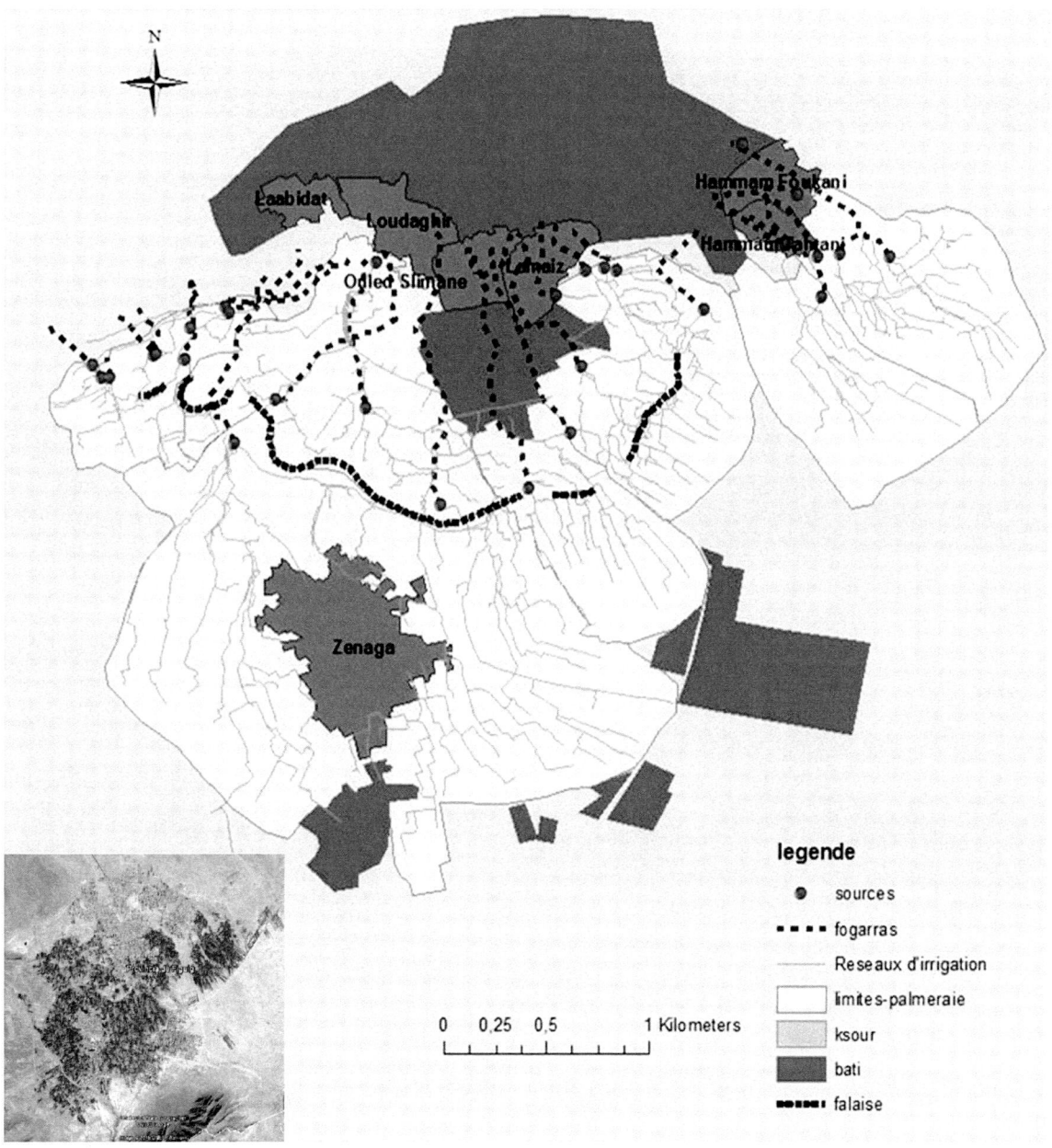

FIGURE 2. MAP OF THE FIGUIG KSOUR (FROM PASTOR ET AL. 2012: 133);
INSET: SATELLITE IMAGE OF FIGUIG OASIS (GOOGLE MAPS).

existence of these oasis is probably a result of geological processes that trapped fossil water between impermeable layers, and that happen to surge in those places (Gautier, 1905, 1915; Bencherifa and Popp, 1990, Seva *et al.* 2012: 43). This water is channeled to and distributed on the surface by a *foggaguir* system, underground conduits that bring fossil water to the surface to feed multiple canals, which irrigate the many walled gardens where palm trees, as well as different sort of fruit trees and vegetables, have been grown for a long time, since the existence of the oasis as a sedentary settlement[1]. Thus, irrigation is still of primary importance for the survival of those who have not elected migration as a subsistence strategy (Figure 3).

---

[1] It is important to mention that the traditional irrigation system has suffered several changes along time as for example the use of electric pumps in some areas, a topic that is not the subject here, for hence will not be further analyzed here.

FIGURE 3. WALLED GARDENS AT FIGUIG OASIS (AUTHOR'S PHOTOGRAPH, DECEMBER 2014).

Several millennia ago, the Figuig desert area was inhabited by hunter-gatherers, as well as pastoral and agro-pastoral societies, when the Sahara was still green, as attested by many rock engravings and paintings that depict extinct animals and scenes of pastoral societies, as well as different archaeological remains as Tumuli, among others. Although there is no accurate information about the origin of Figuig as a sedentary settlement, historical data suggest that some Amazigh (or Berber) tribes, specifically those called zeneta by Ibn Khaldun, were its founders in early Islamic times (see Bencherifa and Popp, 1990:28-30 and Vallat, 2014). Nevertheless, the oasis was never inhabited by a single ethnic or religious group, and although today most of the oasis population is of Amazigh (Berber) origin that profess Muslim faith, Jews, Arabs and Africans (dark skinned people from Sudanese or other south Saharan origins) have been part of the oasis population from remote times, although they always constituted a minority. Likewise, different peoples of various ethnic origins developed many kinds of symbiotic relations with Figuig inhabitants through history. When the French protectorate established its administration in Figuig, a Christian French population came to live there, though later, with the Moroccan independence, these left the oasis leaving only their material traces.

Ibn Khaldun refers to the North African desert in the XIV century as an area journeyed by many different groups, whose way of life was predominantly nomadic, and who differentiate each other by ethnic affiliation, but specially, by the particularities of the animals they owned, a topic linked with the economic activities that they developed to survive. Some of them had dromedaries, others sheep, cattle, horses for breeding, riding and eating (Ibn Khaldun, [1377] 1962:110), and surely many of them had a combination of these; consequently, they were engaged in agro-pastoralism and long distance trade activities.

Thus, each people followed different desert routes and developed distinct relations with the environment, as well as various uses of its resources. Annual nomadic cycles were related to the endurance and the needs of the animals, an important issue that, as mentioned above, used to determine the economic activities of each group that, perhaps since the introduction of the camel by the Romans in the first century, became mainly centered in the trade of valuable wares.

The region south of the Sahara provided grains, salt, ostrich feathers, gold, indigo dye, while tea, sugar and cotton came from the Mediterranean; on the other hand, silk, spices, perfumes and incenses were brought from the Middle East (Claudot-Hawad, 2002:26). But nomad societies often complemented long-distance trade and pastoral economy with robbery of travelers and war pillage. Even if caravan trade constituted an important bridge that allowed communication between distant lands (Claudot-Hawad, 2002:28), in this historical context, the trade routes were like a big ocean with many dangers to overcome before arriving to the secure islands of fortified urban settlements.

This condition prevailed for many different historical periods as observed by many travelers and historians. Speaking specifically about the journey to Figuig, Abi al-Abas al-Hilali al-Sijilmasi, who stopped in Figuig while traveling as a pilgrim to Mecca in the early 1700s, mentions that a group of the nomadic Arab tribe Alumuwr (whose descendants still practice agro-nomadism around the oasis, but slowly became sedentary inhabitants of Moroccan cities), robbed some of his travel companions, but gave back the robbed goods later, perhaps because their victims were in pilgrimage to Mecca (Buwziyan, 2012:115). Therefore, as many trails were uninhabited land, travelers used to buy protection from warrior tribes, or, in some cases, acquired a safe-conduct granted by a tribal chief, to travel through some lands controlled by particular tribes (Hart, 2006:15-31). This observation is valid for Islamic and precolonial Morocco, because, as attested by some historians, the Moroccan dynasties were always involved in political changes and were constantly engaged in war against each other, and consequently did not have a strong and stable organization to control all Moroccan territories. The French and Spanish protectorate in Morocco started in 1912, and the occupation formally finished with Morocco's independence in 1956. Nevertheless, 'tribal pacification', as it was called by the French military, was achieved in different periods in each area. At Figuig oasis, the French did not take total control of the region until 1930.

Socio-political organization and architecture

The socio-political system, called 'Muslim State' by Gellner, was a town-based and religious legitimated monarchy with concentric circles of privileged, autonomous and dissident tribes. Its administration was based on either a peripatetic court and army, or the recognition of local power-holders, rather than corps of bureaucratic nominees (Gellner, 1969:6).

As attested by architectural and archaeological analysis, as well as historical accounts, we can ascertain that Figuig was settled by a group of autonomous confederated tribes that, according to Gellner´s model, were part of the periphery of the several Moroccan Muslim States that succeeded each other during precolonial times. Mountain and desert areas were inhabited also by other autonomous tribes which, in the best case scenario, respected and recognized the Sultan as a religious leader, but not as a political chief.

Anne Levinck, a French traveler who visited Figuig by the end of 1800s, mentions that 'the imperial action of the Sultan' consisted in sending, each year, an officer to levy tax from the Figuig inhabitants; but, most of the time, although this officer was received with great honor, he failed in its principal mission, collecting no tax for the Sultan (Levinck, 1882:17). Though many powerful Moroccan dynasties were enriched by controlling the trade routes, particularly the gold trade routes that connected the Sudan region with the Mediterranean ports, the control of this territory represents only a small part of the large Moroccan land (Boone, Myers and Redman, 1990).

In these conditions, most tribal sedentary societies used to be composed by at least one warrior lineage, or needed to form alliances with some nomadic tribes to be protected (Gellner and Munson, 1995), or otherwise counted with some war specialist that lead battles when necessary. Thus, fortified settlements (as well as defensive strategies) were indispensable to survive in ancient Morocco's oases. Consequently, most part of villages and cities were surrounded by high walls and watchtowers, or as attested by many mountainous towns in the Rif and the Atlas mountains, the settlements were placed in strategic sites that were of difficult access to foreigners.

Figure 4. Ancient earthen watchtowers and rest of a defensive wall at Figuig Oasis (Author's photograph, December 2014).

Even if the oasis constituted fortified urban complexes, we cannot imagine them as isolated villages or cities, but as places where many different ideologies mixed with each other. Nomad and sedentary people developed symbiotic relations over time, exchanging many different wares and perhaps, several notions. Frontiers, as we know them today, are something that do not exist in ancient times, it is probably that big population movements had a general impact in diverse culture areas.

To conclude this section, when analyzing architecture from the archaeological and historical point of view, on one hand, we can affirm the existence of local traditions, but in other hand, we must recognize that these 'local traditions' were enriched with foreign elements. However, external influence seems to have been adapted to a local cultural core that could be attested by the existence of a sociopolitical organization that prevailed before the French intervention of 1912, and, even if it has suffered some changes (whose particularities will not be mentioned here), its main features survive nowadays. This type of sociopolitical organization is known in anthropology as a segmentary system, a model that, in my opinion, could be helpful to understand socio-political organization from an archaeological and historical view, particularly when the analysis focuses on settlementpattern (Figure 4).

Segmentary organization

A segmentary socio-political organization could be defined as a 'tree structure', composed by a number of groups (theoretically similar in strength and size), which in turn are subdivided into smaller corporate groups forming an assemblage with several levels. In Moroccan anthropological studies focused on traditional socio-political organization (see for example Gellner, 1969 and Hart, 1976), the highest levels of the 'tree structure' are usually called tribe, the smaller branches of the 'tree' are clans and sub clans, and finally, the lowest level is known as lineage. In this oasis sedentary context, the tribe (or the *taqbilt,* as called locally in Figuig Amazigh/Berber language) is represented by the fortified urban unit built of earth, calledIn Amazigh (Berber) from Figuig, *aghrem* (pl. *igherman*) (Benamara, 2013: 186, 523-524).[2]

---

[2] Or *ighrem* in other areas of southern Morocco, a term translated as town or city in French (ville or cité), and equate, by the first Arabs who arrived in the region, with the word *ksar* (which plural is *ksour),* that is a reference not to a complete urban settlement, but to a single castle or fortress. Therefore, even if the Arabic term is better known in academic studies, *aghrem* seems to be the more appropriate (Benamara, 2013:186,522-523 and Laoust, 1920:2).

Nevertheless, the corporate groups are not always constituted by lineages, therefore, a 'segmentary system' should not be confused with a 'lineage segmentary system', a theoretical model that does not fit exactly with a social reality where corporate groups exist in many different combinations, linked by affinities that, in some cases, are more important than kin ties. The corporate group can rarely be inferred in archaeological record, but household compounds usually represent lineages, based on ethnographic record.

Anyway, whatever the bases that link a corporate group, the central feature of a segmentary system is the lack of a bureaucratic apparatus and the absence of a single leader that head a government, because there is no government institution, as defined in a centralized organization. It means that, in this type of societies, institutions responsible for the maintenance of order, the management of the means of production (as for example water management) and the control of labor, do not exist. In short, there is no bureaucratic apparatus of any kind, all order maintenance and resource management is under the responsibility of particular corporate groups that constitute branches of the 'tree structure' (see Gellner, 1969:41-49).

Speaking in terms of archaeological and architectural analysis, every settlement is in principle built in accordance with its sociopolitical and religious organization. Thus, in a segmentary society, we should not expect to find buildings destined for a bureaucratic apparatus, and no palaces for any type of single ruler or king. Such settlements shall show no evidence of a single group controlling the means of production.

Nonetheless, the absence of a government and institutions responsible for the maintenance of order, does not mean to live in disorder. Usually those type of societies, particularly in nomadic contexts, have unwritten moral and legal codes and rituals, well established and recognized by all members of community. In sedentary contexts, those legal codes were usually written down in a certain historical moment.

In those societies, when any kind of conflict arises, it involves corporate groups and not individuals as in Western society. Depending on the severity and the type of conflict, the resolution can involve only the lower levels of the tree structure (lineages or other type of corporate groups), or the intervention of the elder council that represents the higher level of the 'tree structure' (the tribe) (see Gluckman, 2009 [1955]:16). In the first case, the resolution of any dispute is carried out only by verbal agreement between the corporate groups involved in the problem. Logically, this type of resolution does not have any material correspondence. But in the second case, the resolution is written and signed by the members of the elder council. In Figuig, a copy of documents that contain those resolutions are stored in a particular building called the *Jma'a* (a term that refers also to the elder council),[3] a particular building placed beside the mosque where some council meetings take place. Of course, some of the changes that took place along time, involve distinct legal changes due to imposition of colonial and Moroccan government authorities, and, speaking in architectural terms, the addition of new buildings for a bureaucracy and European style houses for particular functionaries, regularly built outside the ancient nuclei of the *aghrem*; nevertheless, this is a large topic and for hence, it will not be further analyzed here.

In a traditional, independent, sedentary segmentary society, the settlement pattern analysis predicts an absence of buildings for a specialized bureaucracy, and this is one of the most relevant characteristics of this type of society. In such cases, the settlement of interest should have an open area for assembly meetings, or a unique building where these activities take place. As noted, this is the case of Figuig, but not of all segmentary Amazigh (Berber) and Arab societies from Morocco. However, an important element of most segmentary Moroccan systems, includes the role of holy men (*shurfa*) that come from a lineage claiming to descend from the Prophet Mohamed. A particular man of these holy

---

[3] *Agrar* isthe Amazigh word that refers to the elder council (Benamara, 2013:523), but here we prefer the Arabic term due to its wide local use.

lineages usually acts as leader of a *zāwīyah*[4] (religious order) and plays the role of a 'professional neutral', who arbitrates the conflicts that involve distinct groups of the 'tree structure', or, in a higher structural level, between distinct tribes. The *shurfa's* intervention is needed when a specific quarrel exceeds the functions of the elder council.

At Figuig, as in most Moroccan tribes, the traditional segmentary system (before the French intervention) was complemented by 'holy professional neutrals', as Ernest Gellner calls them (see Gellner 1969). In terms of settlement pattern analysis, the residence of the *zāwīyah*, theoretically, should be located in neutral areas, but this is not always the case. However, if a *zāwīyah* is placed beside the *Jma'a*, it doesn't mean that the *zāwīyah's* leader was always a member of the elder council, because, as told above, his function was to arbitrate when a quarrel exceeds the elder council. This is not the case of the Imam, who in past times (mainly before the Moroccan Independence) was always a member of the *Jma'a*, which is why the mosque and the Qur'anic school are usually placed beside the *Jma'a* building. For that reason, the Imam should not be confused with the 'holy arbitrators' mentioned above (see Ramírez, 2013, Cornell, 1998 and Gellner, 1969). Thus, a 'segmentary architectural complex' could not be complete without a great plaza where the people could listen to the resolutions and announcements of the elder council.

Another relevant characteristic of the ancient settlement pattern of the Figuig *aghrem* is the repetitive layout in each part of the *aghrem*. It means that if an *aghrem* represents a 'tribe' (the higher level of the 'tree structure'), the larger internal divisions defined by high walls with a few, guarded accesses, represent the clans with their sub clans and lineages. Each *aghrem* has a 'segmentary architectural complex' that, as defined here, contains the following elements: 1) a particular building called the *Jma'a*, where some meetings of the elder council take place and the few properties of the *Jma'a* (the elder council) are stored (including the written legal codes and a copy of the documents that contain the resolutions of quarrels); 2) the Mosque, placed in a space that usually includes some seats its entrance, used by the members of the Jma'a); 3) the Qur'anic school, and, 4) a great plaza that also serves commercial activities. In the clan compounds of an *aghrem*, we can find a replication of some of the first three elements mentioned above. Sometimes the fourth element is also repeated, but it is not a rule. Those elements could be different in size and design, but not in function; the differences may due to the relative political importance of the clans that composed a tribe. The *Jma'a* of a tribe is composed by a number of elders that divide in groups that represent clans. For example, the elder council at Loudaghir *aghrem* in Figuig is composed by twelve members, each group of three represent a clan that had their own *Jma'a* building at the center of their urban unit (a quarter of the *aghrem* that represent a clan).

Urban settlement pattern as proxy of segmentary systems

This tribal 'segmentary architectural complex' and the elements of it that were replicated in the lowest levels of the tree structure (which may have some variations depending on the cultural particularities of the society analyzed), is, in my opinion, the nuclear element that serves in an archaeological settlement pattern analysis to define a segmentary system. Yet, sometimes there are other elements that do not fit in this 'architectural complex', but even that does not alter the sociopolitical organization. One of those elements in Figuig is, for example, the Jewish synagogues that could be placed in front, or beside, a mosque (only three *ighreman*, Ouled Sliman, Zenaga and Loudaghir, were inhabited by a minority of Jew population). As we know by historical references, the Jewish community of an *aghrem* chose one of its member to represent their community at the *Jma'a*, and this person could be, indistinctly, a religious or a lay man; thus, to be a Jewish religious leader, does not necessary means -in the context of the segmentary system-, to be responsible of any particular role in the

---

[4] The Arabic term *zāwīyah* refers to a religious lodge, or to a particular building associated to a religious order. It can be a place dedicated to teach the Quran, or an area destined to meditation and prayer. Gellner signals that a *zāwīyah* is different in the urban milieu than in the countryside, where the concept refers not only to a special building, but to a holy lineage (Gellner, 1969:8).

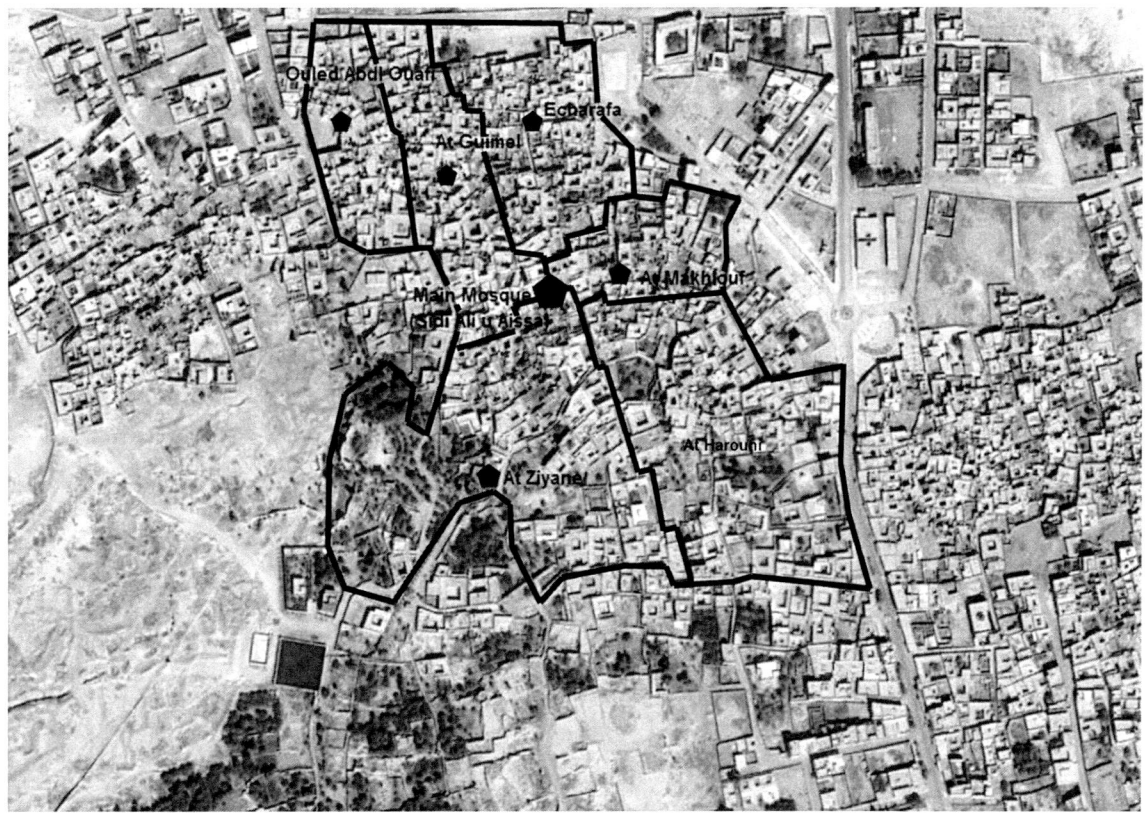

FIGURE 5. SETTLEMENT PATTERN IN THE OLD CENTER OF THE FIGUIG KSOUR
(SATELLITE IMAGE MODIFIED BY THE AUTHOR, GOOGLE EARTH).

Jma'a. Therefore, the placement of a synagogue in front of a mosque could be interpreted, perhaps, as a symbol of the good relations that Muslims -the owners of the land- and Jews -the foreigners that were welcomed by the Muslims- had in past times (for historical references of the Jewish population see Vallat, 2014).

This sense of 'spatial order', that place at the center of an *aghrem*, all the political buildings, was repeated when it was necessary to carry out a big meeting between the elder councils of each *aghrem*. Large assemblies took place, at least, since the end of XIX century as observed by Anne Levinck who mentions that four times a year, the eight *igherman* of Figuig (the number of *igherman* has changed through time), performed a big assembly. It was 'the time of the *Jma'a*', as she called it. These big meetings that fit together each *aghrem* council (or *aghrem Jma'a*), took place in the center of the oasis, in a particular site declared as neutral, under large wool tents (Levinck, 1882:16).

Within the old center of Figuig, the settlement pattern reflects this segmentary pattern of organization. The small pentagons in the satellite image (Figure 5) show the mosques at the center of their ancient area of the *aghrem*, where the elder council still has political influence. The main Mosque (large pentagon) represents the central place of the ancient segmentary system. Some factions used to form one quarter (a corporate group) as is the case of At Guimel, formed by Tachraft lineage and Ouled Abdl Ouafi (Si Moustafa Isawi, personal communication, November 2014), but corporate groups, or factions, were not the same along history, therefore, each faction may have had a mosque that functioned as a *Jmaa* meeting place in the past, when they acted as individual factions.

Besides the special function buildings, each *aghrem* will have a large number of household compounds, made up of individual households, walled gardens, irrigation network, covered passageways that connect all the population of this particular *aghrem*. etc., nevertheless, because of the vastness and particularities of each issue, these will not to be examined in detail here. Yet, the conjunction of the different household compounds and special buildings repeats itself in all the *igherman*, thus reflecting the segmentary relation in the architecture. We will continue this short analysis with a brief mention of the link between socio-political organization and the building techniques and materials.

Segmentary social organization and collective labor

The segmentary organization of a given society will also be reflected in building techniques and collective labor, a topic that could be developed in various levels depending on the complexity of the settlement analyzed. In Figuig, each *aghrem* is composed by different buildings which differ in degrees of quality.

Religious and political buildings have a more complex layout and a finer architectural design and workmanship than the one observed in household compounds and garden areas. In a segmentary society, all the labor needed to build and maintain, year by year, these earthen buildings, will be provided by communal collective labor. In North African Amazigh (Berber) societies, collective labor strategies that permit to undertake major projects, are called *tawiza* in all Amazigh languages.

Each area of an *aghrem* needs a different labor input and degree of specialization, in consequence, each area requires a particular analysis. A general observation related to earthen architecture is that, although this traditional architecture has enormous advantages in comparison with modern designs and materials, as for example the thermic qualities of earth when used as building material and the free and plentiful availability of the natural raw materials, among others. However, one of the negative aspects of this earthen architecture is that it needs a higher labor input that, without a segmentary system that can provide this labor 'for free', raises the cost and maintenance of these buildings to the level of exceeding largely the cost of cement and other modern materials. This, combined with migration and ideological changes, are factors that impacts directly with earthen conservation issues.

Many different efforts to conserve and rehabilitate several earthen buildings have been carried out by many local and foreign associations. Nevertheless, the destruction brought about by the strong rains that lashed Figuig during November 2014, shows that without an efficient *tawiza* system, the earthen architecture conservation is, perhaps, impossible. During that exceptional downpour, the ancient earthen nuclei of all Figuig *aghrem* and garden areas suffered enormous damages that needed the urgent intervention of the elder assemblies to organize different *tawiza* working days to repair walls, canals and households which, in some cases, were completely demolished by the rain.

I had the opportunity to observe how the *Jma'a* of *aghrem* Loudaghir, after few days of absolutely chaos (when a big number of families moved to a municipal refuge, while the road that links Figuig and Oujda was blocked by the swollen rivers), implemented a *tawiza* party to clean the garden areas. This strategy will be repeated as many times as necessary.

As in other egalitarian systems, each lineage head that possesses a parcel in the garden area, no matter if he is a member of the *Jma'a*, a Moroccan government functionary, or just a farmer, must participate equally in the *tawiza*. At that time the *Jma'a* choose the Sunday, a day off, so lineage heads would have the opportunity to participate in collective works. If one of the lineage heads were unable to work on this day, it will be his responsibility to send a worker, paid by his lineage, to take his place. Then, on that Sunday, most of garden areas were cleaned, while walls and canals were waiting for the next *tawiza* to be completely repaired. In the same way, all other areas of the *aghrem* will be rehabilitated in a collective effort between government authorities, civil associations and Loudaghir inhabitants through its traditional *tawiza*.

Conclusions

I have cited a small example of *tawiza* linked with an earthen architecture conservation issue to show that traditional architecture cannot be considered only an issue of tangible cultural heritage, but as an issue that links tangible and intangible cultural heritage. Thus, all strategies to study and conserve earthen architecture at Figuig, must include the traditional socio-political organization, its values, collective principles and social rules, that constituted themselves through time but are now progressively being lost, a heritage that should be protected in the same way as the traditional earthen architecture. Besides, this *tawiza* example shows us how communal collective labor was necessary in past times to give rise to those fortified earthen urban units that serve as secure fortified posts when the Sahara was journeyed by several caravan traders, pilgrims and travelers since early Islamic times.

Acknowledgements

This paper could not have been written without the kind assistance of Dr. Hassan Aouraghe, Dr. Annick Daneels, Mr. Amar Abbou, Mr. Tayeb Jabri, Mr. Ouajd Karkar, Si Moustafa Isawi (an honorable member of the *aghrem* Loudaghir elder council), as well as many of the inhabitants of Figuig who kindly shared with me valuable information related to their cultural heritage. Also, it is important to mention that since November 2014 the research is financed by the Mexican institution CONACYT (*Consejo Nacional de Ciencia y Tecnología*), in the context of their annual fellow postdoctoral program. In addition, I want to express my gratitude to Figuig Municipality that kindly provides me with lodging during the field research in 2013, 2014 and 2015.

Bibliography

BENCHERIFA, A.; POPP, H. 1990. L'Oasis de Figuig, Persistance et Changement, Publication de la Faculté des Lettres et des Sciences Humaines de Rabat, Série Essais et Études N. 3, Rabat: Royaume du Maroc, Université Mohamed V. 109 p.

BENAMARA, H. 2013. Dictionnaire Amazighe – Français, Parler de Figuig et ses régions, Centre de l'Aménagement Linguistique UER-Lexique, Rabat: Institut Royale de la Culture Amazighe. 784 p.

BOONE, J.; EMLEN, L.; MYERS, J.; REDMAN, CH. 1990. Archaeological and Historical Approaches to Complex Societies: The Islamic State of Medieval Morocco. American Anthropologist, New Series, Vol. 92, No. 3, September, 630-646 p.

BUWZIYAN, B. M. 2012. Al-tawğih li-Bayt Al-llah Al-harām wa-ziyārah qabrih ʿalayhi al-ṣalāh wa-al-salām. Riḥlah Abī Al-ʿAbās Al-Hilālī al-Siğilmāsī (Towards the House of God [Mecca] and visit to the Prophet's tomb. The peace be with him. Travel of Abi Al-Abas al-Hilali al-Sijilmasi). Figuig Cultural Heritage n. 10 – Oujda: Al Josor. 196 p.

CLAUDOT-HAWAD, H. 2007. Touaregs, Apprivoiser le désert.Paris: Découvertes Gallimard. 143 p.

CORNELL, V. 1998. Realm of the Saint, Power and Authority in Moroccan Sufism. Austin: University of Texas Press. 424 p.

GELLNER, E. 1969. Saints of the Atlas, London: Weidenfeld and Nicolson. xxiii+317 p.

GELLNER, E.; MUNSON, H. JR. 1995. Segmentation: Reality or Myth? The Journal of the Royal Anthropological Institute, Vol. 1, No. 4 (Dec.), p. 821-832 [Consult. 10 Oct. 2012]. Available at URL: http://www.jstor.org/stable/3034963

GLUCKMAN, M. 2009) [1955] – Costumbre y Conflicto en África, Lima: Universidad Nacional de San Marcos, Fondo Editorial UCH. 198 p.

HART, D. M. 2006. Bandidismo en el Islam: Estudios de Caso en Marruecos, Argelia y la Frontera Noroeste de Pakistan. Barcelona: Anthropos. 121 p.

IBN KHALDUN (1962) [1377] – The Muqaddimah, Translated by Franz Rosenthal. [Consult. 6 Sept. 2014] Available at URL: http://asadullahali.files.wordpress.com/2012/10/ibn_khaldun-al_muqaddimah.pdf

Laoust, E. 1920. Mots et Choses Berbères, Notes de linguistique et d'Ethnographie, Dialectes du Maroc, Paris: A. Challamel, XX-531 p.

Levinck, A. 1882. L'Oasis de Figuig. Paris: Revue de Geographie I.G.P. 26 p.

Pastor-López, A. *et al.* 2012. Los Palmerales de Figuig (Marruecos) Y Elche (España). Comparación estructural Y ecológica. Patrones de degradación Y gestión sostenible / Les Palmeraies de Figuig (Maroc) et Elche (Espagne). Comparaison estructurel et ecologique. Schemas de dégradation et aménagement durable. In Vargas-Llovera, M. D., *et al.* (Eds.), Bases ecológicas y culturales del oasis de Figuig (Marruecos) / Fondations écologiques et culturelles de l'oasis Figuig (Maroc). Oujda: Proyecto de Cooperación Internacional al Desarrollo AP/301-34-2010 de AECID and Facultad de Letras y Humanidades de la Universidad Mohamed VI de Oujda. [Consult. 24 Nov. 2014] Available at URL: http://rua.ua.es/dspace/bitstream/10045/26155/1/7%20Antonio%20Pastor.pdf

Ramírez-Rodríguez, F. T. A. U. 2013. Los 'Santos' (Imrabḍen) y el paisaje cultural entre los Ayt Ali u Aissa (Ayt Σli u Σissa) del Rif Central Marroquí desde una perspectiva etnoarqueológica. PhD dissertation Archaeological Studies (Estudios Arqueológicos). México: ENAH (Escuela Nacional de Antropología e Historia). 381 p.

Seva-Roman, E.; Martin-Martin, J.; Pastor-Lopez, A. 2012. Construcción de un Sistema de Información Geográfica Válido para el Estudio Integrado del Oasis de Figuig. In Vargas-Llovera, M. D., Seva-Román, E. and Hamdaoui, M. (Eds.), Bases Ecológicas y Culturales del Oasis de Figuig (Marruecos) / Fondations Écologiques et Culturelles de l'Oasis Figuig (Maroc). Oujda: Published by Proyecto de Cooperación Internacional al Desarrollo AP/301-34-2010 de AECID, and Facultad de Letras y Humanidades de la Universidad Mohamed VI de Oujda.

Vallat, J.-P. (Ed.) 2014. Le Patrimoine Marocain: Figuig une Oasis au Cœur des Cultures. Paris: L'Harmattan, 488 p.